Oriental Architecture/1

Mario Bussagli

Oriental Architecture/1

India, Indonesia, Indochina

Translated by John Shepley

Contribution by
Arcangela Santoro

Electa/*Rizzoli* NEW YORK

Photographs: Federico Borromeo
Drawings: Studio Enzo di Grazia
Layout: Arturo Anzani

Library of Congress Cataloging in Publication Data

Bussagli, Mario.
    Oriental architecture.

    (History of world architecture)
    Translation of: Architettura orientale.
    Bibliography: p.
    Includes index.
    Contents: 1. India, Indonesia, Indochina —
2. China, Korea, Japan.
    1. Architecture, Oriental. I. Title. II. Series:
History of world architecture (Electa/Rizzoli)
NA1460.B8713 1989 722   88-43458
ISBN 0-8478-1056-9 (v. 1) (pbk.)
ISBN 0-8478-1055-0 (v. 2) (pbk.)

TABLE OF CONTENTS

The publication of a work devoted solely to the architecture of central and eastern Asia clearly reflects the new interest in the artistic culture of those great Asian civilizations that—by a possibly controversial definition—may also be called "Far Eastern." *Oriental Architecture* brings together and synthesizes in one work the architectural developments of seven large regions—all of them marked by complex historical vicissitudes, by equally complicated social phenomena, and by an extraordinary richness of thought. The customary rule is to compile a separate volume for each cultural area, or at least to devote one volume to each of the major cultures of these regions. There are, however, in addition to certain contingent and absolute requirements that preclude these alternatives, theoretical and scientific reasons, which are set forth more fully in the Introduction, that justify a unified treatment of the architectural works here examined. Above all, there exist undeniable ties and relationships that link together these highly diverse artistic cultures.

The attentive reader will soon discern the nature of the more obvious of these relationships—which do not reside merely in matters of type or technique, or in the predominant use of particular materials, since these are often of a religious and spiritual character—as well as the existence of minor but widely radiating currents of taste, and of influences and pressures. The latter, while sometimes involving countries very remote from one another, have nevertheless served to produce a dense network of lesser ties that evidence what we might call the "differentiated unity" of Asia.

The contributors to this work (all teachers at the University of Rome) are Italian scholars with varying backgrounds—linguistics, history, art history—whose interest in the study of the figurative arts in Asia has been inspired by their specialties. They all bring to their respective discussions the enrichment of the particular studies in which they have participated. The result is a kind of *concordia discors* that in part corresponds to the objective requirements of the individual fields of the contributors, who will sometimes emphasize rhythms of development, at other times historical conditions, spatial values, or technical data, according to their sensibilities, their preferences, and even their basic training. Moreover, it was no easy task to confront the problems of Asian architecture and to remove them from the accompanying art historical context of the other figurative arts; throughout Asia, architecture is considered a minor art and is not always easily separated from sculpture and, to a lesser degree, from painting.

There have even been serious difficulties in the choice of illustrations. Except for Federico Borromeo's photographs, taken especially for this work with a skill that is not merely technical but also that of an enthusiastic lover of Asian (especially Indian) art, it was no easy matter to collect suitable, new, and previously unpublished material. On the other hand, in some regions—such as Central Asia—there has been scant survival of significant monuments; what little remains can in no way be compared with the wealth of other areas. The well-known political conditions in such countries as Vietnam have hindered specific photographic projects, and consequently there is a considerable disproportion between the visual documentation for some regions and other richer and more accessible ones.

Despite these handicaps, this work represents a necessary preparatory move toward wider and deeper investigations that, among other things, will inevitably have to confront the problem of figurative space in the Asian world. On the formulation of this problem—by no means easy because it collides with the entire history of art of the adjoining European continent, and with scientific and philosophical conceptions elaborated by individual civilizations—depends the possibility of a single basic critical standard, one common to such highly different worlds and capable of bringing research on the artistic phenomena of Europe and Asia to the same level. It is now time for the history of art to become a single history—even though cultivated by specialists in diverse regions of the world—with similar (if not necessarily identical) problems, views, and methods, differentiated only by the diversity of documentary evidence and by the methods employed in approaching aesthetic values.

Final judgment on this work is naturally up to its readers, whether they be specialists or not, and the books' fate is primarily entrusted to them. For us, as authors, it is already a satisfaction to be able to offer and reveal to a wider public the architectural treasures of civilizations that have developed parallel to our own, and which represent not its antithesis but its completion and its reciprocal parameter of measure.

Mario Bussagli

The characteristic forms of Asian architecture are still one of the most striking and familiar aspects of the artificial "Oriental" world that our increased knowledge and facility in mass communication cannot successfully eliminate. The taste for the fantastic and exotic, however slight today, may be said to be ingrained in the human spirit, and for historical reasons is particularly felt by Western man. The Great Wall of China, any of the pagodas of the Far East, the stupas of India and the Indianized world, the great temples of China, Japan, and Southeast Asia—all evoke an indefinable sense of wonder, a mysterious and diverse presence that shapes itself in a primarily emotional way, even though its effect upon us has been given lucid literary expression by a number of our best writers. But an evaluation of this kind, which we might call sentimental-exotic, remains a superficial one, and is in any case the fruit of a European-centered view, or at least extraneous to the very world that produced the monuments of which we speak. In reality, these and an infinite number of other architectural works reflect the social, economic, and historical structure of an immense and varied world, subject to transformations that are no less felt for being slow and conflicting. The sum of the Asian experiments, the series of critical problems faced, and the variety of technical results obtained thereby are not inferior to those that have ripened over the centuries in the West, even though there is a general tendency to contrast Asian architecture with what is vaguely and generically defined as Western.

In no Asian civilization has architecture ever been considered one of the major arts. The heaviness of the materials employed, and the quantity of technical data necessary for planning and construction, have led to the conclusion that it is hardly spontaneous, not easily appreciated, and therefore the product of the craftsman rather than a work of art. Thus, the technical texts of India—to begin with, the *Mānasāra*, which though late is one of the most complete—enumerate with great precision the various aspects of the technical training necessary for the architect. These include geology, geometry, magic, religion, artistic techniques, and even psychology (the latter to assist in dealing with workers). Indeed, the whole implies a specialized body of learning that is certainly uncommon and quite different from that of Western classical or Renaissance architects, not to mention any modern or contemporary ones.

In the Far Eastern world, where wood is deliberately employed and architectural forms are placed within the sphere of nature—one thinks of gardens and of the Sino-Japanese ability to exploit the natural surroundings of a building—the architectural work takes its place on a lower scale in a hierarchy of artistic values wherein painting, calligraphy, poetry, and music stand at the top. In recent decades, Far Eastern concepts and techniques have been translated, with considerable freedom, into new and strikingly contemporary architectural terms, even calling for materials absolutely different from the ancient and traditional wooden structures. Through a combination of varying circumstances, the traditions of Japan and the renewed creative capacities of her great contemporary architects have produced vast echoes in Europe and America. A great part of this sincere interest is due to the efforts of Japanese architects to reconcile the significance and continuity of their tradition with the inevitable change and updating of their culture, which is driven by an urge to create new symbols and new common values acceptable to a spiritually, economically, and socially reinvigorated world.

That these efforts are perfectly justified and valid is an undeniable fact; consequently, the entire span of Asian architecture cannot be judged merely as an historical and archaeological phenomenon, nor should we study its works as a simple heritage of the past. With the fluctuations and continual variations in the scales of values adopted by all human civilizations, it can still be a source of suggestions and of possible inspiration (likewise for experiments unknown to the Western world), and it may well be capable of future developments. In any case—setting aside historically documented amalgamations of East and West—there can be no doubt whatsoever that the Asian experience remains a parameter of comparison for the architecture of other continents. To recognize it as such will enrich our historical and aesthetic vision, and among other things will help us to confront the question of the allegedly irreconcilable opposition between Asia and Europe in the architectural sphere.

But is it really legitimate to speak of an Asian architecture? The various artistic civilizations of Asia display enormous differences among themselves, and the response of Asian man is likewise different in varying climatic and environmental situations. As a result, the vast series of socio-cultural phenomena and their related reflections in architecture as manifested during centuries and millennia would seem to deny the methodological correctness of a unified treatment. To judge by appearances, an approach of this sort can be justified only by a tenuous and debatable geographical bond.

In reality, all of Asia is overlaid by an imposing complex of cultural phenomena that tends to unify its broad areas on partially homogeneous grounds, which in turn are strengthened and extended by mutual influences, contacts, and exchanges. Moreover, the economic and organizational structure of the Asian world, however fractured, obeys a series of common choices and preferences; its architectural works, expressing as they may highly different aspirations and intentions, remain above all unmistakably Asian.

The prejudicial question on which the validity of this essay—and, in part, of those that follow—depends can be answered in the affirmative, since even if one takes note of the aesthetic, functional, or technical differences that separate these works, tastes, and tendencies, it is not difficult to perceive their common foundation and the extensive interplay of mutual influences.

Naturally, in a book such as this, it is necessary ro rely on available sociological data, and to consider also the philological and psychological approaches. The true protagonist of our research is, however, the artistic phenomenon in itself, evaluated and considered both on the sociological (especially symbolic and religious) plane and in its historical and political context, despite the obvious limitations imposed by the almost complete anonymity of the artists involved (particularly in the architectural field) and by the relatively sparse nature of the philological evidence.

The northern stretches of the Asian continent, corresponding to the area of tundras and forests and to part of the central strip of deserts and steppes, were almost completely unacquainted with architecture until very recent times. Only underground tombs of various types (such as chambers or pits), indicated on the surface by rings of stones, tumuli, or in some other manner, demonstrate the existence of a desire to build, obviously prompted by the impulse of sacred and funerary values. Much rarer in occurrence and more recent in date are certain subterranean dwellings that respond to climatic requirements—protection from the cold, for example—and to functional values that can be understood only in terms of a particular religious culture. The marks of shamanism so overload such structures with symbolic values that, once they are divorced from the culture that produced them, the solutions adopted for accessibility, livability, and the very life in common of the hierarchical group served by them are rendered absurd. They are typical examples of a symbolic and magical functionalism so exaggerated as to be an extreme case even for Asia.

Chinese literary sources mention the small fortified "cities" in wood and stone built by certain nomadic groups as they became progressively sedentary under the influence of Chinese culture. No examples have survived, just as almost nothing, except for fragments, remains of the fourteenth-century Catholic churches in Mongolia (in the Gothic style but with ample concessions to Chinese techniques and materials) built by Giovanni di Montecorvino. These scant remains comprise almost the entire architectural heritage of the nomadic peoples and hunters of the north. We must remember, however, that the felt tent of the nomads, a true masterpiece of practicality and rationality, itself reproduced the shamanistic symbolism of underground dwellings, which thus appears as an indispensable requirement.

Apparently, an enormous portion of the Asian continent was for a long time devoid of important architectural forms. Until quite recent times, there were no actual urban agglomerates; we can say that the urbanization of this immense area is connected with the history of the last two centuries and has developed primarily along Russian lines, with considerable intensification in the last few decades.

It is thus the great sedentary, agricultural civilizations of the south—including all the territories of China and Korea, as well as the Japanese archipelago—that have expressed themselves in valid and coherent architectural forms capable of broad development. These forms, when placed according to type and purpose in urban contexts and in very diverse groupings, can be better understood by an examination of the essential outlines of the Asian city.

The Asian City

Throughout Asia the city has had a very different meaning from that it possesses in the West (first, Classical Mediterranean, later European). It is still less important than the village as a human habitat, which is in fact the fundamental agglomerate in all sedentary Asian societies. Apart from the existence of modern megalopolises such as Tokyo, for example, the distribution of the population into hamlets, the tendency toward isolation, the conservatism characteristic of the village, and the continual rapport of man with nature—whose gigantic forces are manifested in Asia with a violence unknown in the West—have not been devoid of consequences in the field of architecture. In Indian villages, for example, the principal construction remained for centuries the Vedic altar, a structure rigidly connected with symbolic requirements, even down to the number of bricks employed, and with ritual function. Concepts of durability, aesthetic value, and rationality in the modern sense have not been taken into consideration, however. This psychological attitude has its repercussions on other aspects of religious architecture. Certain works, intended to serve as votive offerings, are built without any interest either in durability or Vitruvian *firmitas*, and thus assume a meaning that is inconceivable to the West. A Buddhist stupa, solid in construction and lacking interior space, may have been erected for the sole purpose of "acquiring merit"—in other words, to better the fate of the patron and builder in his future lives. If the stupa were to crumble or be demolished immediately after being perfectly completed, this would have no importance, since the act of faith that presided over its construction had already been carried out. For tens of centuries, all of Asia lacked the necessary prerequisites whereby the bourgeois class (artisans and merchants) might have acquired an economic strength that would resolutely reflect the life and functions of the cities. The hostility of the central powers toward the mercantile and craft guilds is amply shown both by Indian texts on political theory—these embrace the idea that the *śreni* (guilds), because of their wealth, constitute the principal danger to the sovereign[1]—and by the Confucian contempt for trade.

As a result, there existed no juridical foundation permitting the formation of civic autonomy and the recognition of the urban community within the outlines of an independent civilization, distinct from the surrounding ones—as occurred, for example, in Italy. In China, the building of a new city was one of a number of works carried out by the state, and the planned urban centers served as an instrument of central power. Their purpose, in fact, was to ensure the transportation, storage, and distribution of principal goods, not to mention their military and internal security functions. Nor could it have been otherwise, since all Chinese imperial governments considered the entire territory under their rule as a unified whole.[2]

What was therefore planned for the Chinese populace was a general system by which they would be distributed throughout cities and lesser centers according to the needs foreseen and imposed by an absolute power—one that, despite being abstract and remote, in theory excluded free activities and had no interest in favoring the city over the village. It was not accidental that inside the cities themselves each quarter was isolated and autonomous in its relations with the local authority. The connection between house and street was bound up in precise rules that, in the more ancient periods of the empire (roughly speaking, from the second century B.C. to the ninth century A.D.), granted free and direct access to the street only to the highest functionaries. The necessity for police control and the desire to shatter any sense of civic unity account for the imposition of a particular physical aspect on the Chinese city that would be unacceptable in other civilizations. Distinguished by the presence of city walls and constructed on a grid plan (confirmed in a later period by Marco Polo's description of Cambaluc, present-day Peking), the urban nucleus was essentially an instrument of oppression. Only under the Sung, at the end of the tenth century, did this significance begin to diminish, even though the central government still remained abstract and remote, circumscribed as it was in its decisions and administrative activity by the sphere of the court. The Mongol invasion was to reduce the importance of the city once more, as a result of the nomadic origins of the new rulers and their characteristically imperial vision with its overtones of universalism.

Something similar happened in India too, where the political division of the immense subcontinent exposed its inhabitants to continual fluctuations in the ruling power because of the expansion and collapse of various state structures. Curiously enough, throughout the centuries and despite complex historical vicissitudes, the only agency to remain firm and operative was the land office, on which the tax yield depended—especially in such an agricultural society *par excellence* as that of India.

There can thus be no doubt that one of the basic characteristics of Asian unity is precisely this complex socio-economic structure that reduces the importance of the city to a minimum, while absolutely excluding the formation of any autonomous powers of an urban kind. Even when the collision with the Islamic world led to the emergence of great Muslim cities, and when coastal centers appeared that were to be Europeanized by commercial expansion, the Asian city was never to achieve autonomy. In short, in no instance did it succeed in expressing any bourgeois strength from its own core. Islam itself, which granted a wider cultural, religious, and administrative importance to the urban nucleus and moved it closer to European examples, was unable to impart a juridical appearance or an operative autonomy to civic centers. The colonialist drive created mercantile and military bases, especially on the coasts, but had neither the aim nor the possibility of reproducing European-style urban structures in Asia for the benefit of the Asians. For the colonial rulers, the city was likewise an instrument of power, though naturally, from their contact with various economic systems, the natives of the surrounding areas were able to derive some advantage.

Thus there arises once again, in relation to the value and function of the Asian city, the much-discussed problem of the "Asian mode of production," which, among other things, is said to constitute one of the undivided and unifying components of Asian society. Actually, this expression, coined by Karl Marx, becomes more precise when defined as a "despotic village economy,"[3] since it is characterized by a combination of the production activity of village communities and the economic intervention of a state authority that exploits and at the same time directs them. There is no doubt, however, that at the root of all sedentary Asian societies there has been maintained, for extremely long periods and in different forms, an interest in public works that the state (or sovereign) provides for and executes. These works are controlled and administered in the same manner as commerce, many mining and refining industries, transportation, and various other activities, with the state (or sovereign) theoretically limiting its own power only in relation to the capacity of its subjects for endurance and survival. This centralization, this despotic authoritarianism, was preserved even when the political acts of the sovereign were based on a humanitarian ideology and formulated according to concepts of universal brotherhood, respect for life, and "nonviolence." Such was the case of Asoka (c. 269-232 B.C.), the third and greatest sovereign of the Maurya dynasty, the first Indian empire. Asoka, who derived the foundations for his own political vision from Buddhist ethics, undertook great public works—streets, hospitals, reservoirs, cisterns, commemorative and symbolic pillars. His was an Asian state, and though paternalistic and only mildly oppressive, was still incapable of breaking the truly tyrannical patterns of his ancestors.

In addition to this pronounced tendency toward centralization, private property and initiative were hindered by all legislative and fiscal means. Thus there existed a basic antagonism between the masses of subjects and the bureaucratic apparatus of the state, making it very obvious why private property did not confer any real political power. It is for this reason that Asian societies, except when they come into violent contact with other, totally different social structures—and in particular with colonialist capitalism—appear almost incapable of rapid development. This does not mean that they are immobile or identical among themselves. Inversely, it is hardly correct to say, as does Chesneaux, that "the theory of Asian society is a myth, rather than a useful scientific hypothesis," it being understood that this theory applies primarily to the more productive agricultural areas. The Central Asian area, in the centuries from the beginning of the Christian era to its total conquest by the Turks (ninth to tenth centuries A.D.) does not enter into Chesneaux's description because the economic basis of the entire region was essentially mercantile. The western area, where greater agricultural development was possible through artificial irrigation, pro-

duced state structures of the semifeudal type or, more precisely, alliances of small semiautonomous potentates under a theoretical authority. The other districts, corresponding to the present Sinkiang region in China, saw the emergence of caravan city-states (each with a different cultural structure) founded on oases. Here human habitation, limited by the hostility of the desert and other obstacles, could not be dispersed in a network of agricultural villages. Very close in its outlook to the medieval European world, Central Asia was the only area to make the city the synthesis of a refined civilization and to develop a kind of bourgeois class. A tangible factor was the decentralization of the monastic complexes, which tended to detach them from the restless life of the urban nucleus, thus confirming the importance of religious thought. Nevertheless, in the entire range of Asian civilizations, this remains an extraordinary and fundamental exception. Despite its militarized and strongly bureaucratic state organizations, this region was the only one capable of developing a very profitable socioeconomic structure and of ensuring that its commercial and cultural activity extended over an enormous territory.

Unfortunately, for various reasons, we cannot trace with precision the genesis of this urban structure, which in the West took shape predominantly in the form of large castles and in the East in actual cities. In the latter area, archaeologists have primarily unearthed monastic agglomerates and religious constructions hewn out of rock, which better survived the vicissitudes of the centuries. With the advance of Islam into the area, even though the mercantile economy that had created the splendor of Central Asian civilization was not wholly destroyed, new urban centers of the Muslim type emerged. They would have a physical character of their own, generally not much different from that of Iranian cities or other regions of the Muslim world. Only Samarkand—the sole great love of Tamerlane—was to have the strange destiny of becoming the capital of an ephemeral empire created simply for its embellishment. We might add, in evaluating the "Asian mode of production" theory in relation to architecture, that another exception is found in the theocracy of Tibet, where the economic structure of the plateau took the form of a mixture of livestock breeding and laborious agriculture within the very framework of a state that, after a phase of kingship, was clearly based on religion and entrusted to monastic hierarchies. Here the Asian mode of production does not take the classical Marxist form (actually derived from the India and China of the nineteenth century); nor does it adhere to the more precise definition stated by Chesneaux, which we have followed while yet proposing certain general characteristics.

We still find the state in Tibet promoting large works (though by means of religious communities), but the development of private property and even the yield from the scarce amount of arable land are hindered by magic and superstition, elements that were backed up by the spiritual authorities. Deep plowing, for example, was prohibited so as not to offend the *klu*, the spirits of the earth—corresponding to the *naga*, or deified serpents of

India—who might in turn revenge themselves on the entire country.

This fragment of medieval civilization, with its mystical and magical setting that has lasted until recent years, has also produced highly valid architectural forms that are without doubt Asian. They are specifically Tibetan as well, and have been erected in relation to a number of diverse elements that take their place within the framework of the lamaistic social order, a strongly hierarchical one albeit along lines that differ considerably from other Asian civilizations.

We can conclude therefore that a critical examination of the Asian mode of production shows that, however vast, it does not appear to be limited in space, since something similar can be found in other areas, and that it most certainly varies in time. Nevertheless, this much-discussed economic phenomenon offers two constant characteristics whose unifying importance cannot be denied—the state's interest in public works, and the relative lack of private property and initiative. For these reasons also, the architecture of Asia appears predominantly religious. Great monumental works could be realized primarily in terms of particular cultural structures, in a world where political theories and the practice of government conferred on the holders of power a single possibility for a dialogue with subject groups; this possibility was limited to the sphere of their common acceptance of metaphysical values, whether magical or religious. In other words, religious faith and religiosity were the only common ground for rulers and subjects. This implies the existence of patterns of thought that tend, independent of the reality of economic drives, to accentuate religious speculation to degrees unknown in the West—this on the basis of a total lack of opposition between the sacred and the profane (since the sacred in itself pervades even the slightest act of daily life) and on the conviction that there exists no definite orthodoxy, every form of religious thought being capable of approaching the truth and leading to salvation.

Whether this last circumstance means the reabsorption of the individual into the energy of the universe, or his survival in one or another of the paradises or "pure" lands imagined by the mystics, has no importance. Rather, what counts is that the reality of religion has, for the Asian world, a consistency and importance greatly superior to what we might find outside that continent. Possibilities for meditation were offered by the dispersion of its inhabitants in the immense network of villages. That unique factor, or the separation of religious souls in monastic agglomerates far from the structures of cities, may—in the immobility of a life devoid of shocks—have facilitated spiritual attitudes that in other worlds would be inconceivable. Furthermore, in this case the underdevelopment of cities would be indirectly responsible for a particular Asian mode of thought—one that certainly varies and is often contradictory if we compare the predominant lines of thinking in this or that civilization, but that is nevertheless diffused from one end of the continent to the other and that is essentially devoted to metaphysical speculation.

It is certain that the underdevelopment of Asian cities acts to exclude such concepts as those of *polis, civitas,* or *commune.* What is lacking is the sense of the fraternal group, exposed to external pressures equally dangerous to all and committed to responding collectively to challenges which, if not met and overcome, would threaten the life of all. With the exception of the Central Asian city-state, this is the characteristic common to the great mass of Asian populations; thus, the Japanese *shimin* is a simple translation for the English word and concept of the "citizen," while *chōnin* ("city dweller") is certainly not the French *citoyen* of Republican fame, and even less an expression interchangeable with the Latin *civis* or Greek *polites.* On the other hand, much as some scholars may try to deny it, the religious component in Asian thought remains the determining one to this day, accentuated as it is by the values derived from paranormal experience, and by a remote and intense stratification of the analysis carried out in the depths of the unconscious since earliest times. In conclusion, there is no doubt that historical materialism is one key by which to grasp forms and phenomena of a history as complex and tumultuous as that of Asia. It is, however, not the only one, much less one that can throw light for us on architectural phenomena of broad significance in which a predominant part is played by the collective unconscious—what the Indians call *prakrti,* or "nature."

The Characteristics of Asian Architecture
We are dealing here with a unique economy that excludes any speculation in the building industry, reduces private initiative, and favors the formation of specialized or semispecialized autonomous groups in building construction. The architecture of Asia assumes a special significance when one considers that the curves of economic profit and semiprofit react on it only partially. External intervention such as the state initiates—which may reflect the faith or pride of a sovereign, the religious devotion of high personages, or the interest of the nobles or high bureaucracy, depending on time and place—or the kind produced by religious communities do not allow for situations similar to those that came to fruition in the Classical, medieval, and Renaissance West. It is obvious that, in a world sincerely and profoundly pervaded by deep religiosity, the desire for art is concentrated on religious works of major importance. Nevertheless, aesthetic considerations also play a part in constructions of purely practical utility, and to a greater extent in expensive dwellings. In medieval Japan, one actually notes an interchange between villas and sacred buildings, as shown, for example, by the monastery containing the *Hōōdō* (phoenix hall): originally a villa belonging to the Fujiwara, it was transformed into a sacred building by the regent Yorimichi of the same family.

Traditionally set into their natural surroundings or embellished with artificial references to nature itself—ponds, miniature gardens, "dry" rock gardens using gravel to symbolize water—the villas and large isolated dwellings of the Far East, especially those in Japan, are enlivened by a highly refined taste. It is here in these buildings that one finds the clearest anticipation of modern architecture. For, as we have already noted, conceptions, models, and construction elements from the Japanese tradition have been taken up and translated into other materials by great modern architects—from Ludwig Mies van der Rohe, Walter Gropius, and Frank Lloyd Wright to the present Japanese masters (not excluding, in some phases, Kenzo Tange himself).

The importance of the religious component invests Asian architecture with a complicated system of symbolic allusions. Its historical development might be traced almost completely on the iconological level and by the iconological method, even though this would reveal only a single (albeit important) aspect of a broader and more complex reality. One must, however, keep in mind that the religious component is not homogeneous. In its enormous vitality, it follows divergent lines and even offers substantial variations within the same current or sect, depending on time and place. The phenomenon, encouraged by the systematic lack of a rigid orthodoxy, is especially evident in the wide expansion of ecumenical religions that have collided with areas dominated by very different civilizations; this happened to Indian Buddhism and Hinduism, Persian Manichaeanism, and other lesser known religious currents. In this light, the presumed immobility of Asia can hardly be said to exist because of the polemical vigor of its innovators and commentators, its teeming sects, and the wealth of its mystical experience—a heritage transmitted to groups very much vaster and more prepared than their Western counterparts to receive it.

But this religious interest, however predominant and in a certain sense the summation of its various cultures, does not bar Asia from other interests and areas of speculation. In the so-called humanistic sciences, a number of ideas and theories systematized by the West in modern times were strikingly anticipated in Asia. In psychoanalysis, linguistics, political theory, in the search for paranormal possibilities, even in many fields of technology, Asia has arrived at astonishing results that the West has been slow in realizing, and in some spheres, we have only begun to acknowledge that our own culture is capable of such awareness.

In the fields of economics, politics, and social organization—taking into account the circumstances we described earlier—one can discern behavior or lines of systematic organization that do not always have a secure ideological basis, that respond from time to time to changing practical needs as well. With no revolutionary impulse, but rather by a slow evolutionary process, these patterns have a profound influence on the most intimate fabric of human society. The effort to single out and define the phenomena to which they give rise is always a difficult one; only rarely does it succeed in providing exhaustive data for modern methodological research. But it has been possible to glimpse ancient economic and ecological crises due to overproduction, problems of minting, monetary circulation,[4] inflation, devaluation, stockjobbing, the planned hoarding of gold or silver coins in

contrast to the bimetallic intercontinental circulation of coins that prevailed until the first century A.D. Thus, there is an immense sector of activity, thought, and organization that barely emerges from the available documents. We can attribute this to the nature of the documents themselves (based as they are on patterns of thought, and with intentions foreign to everything that might interest modern specialists in these fields), the chronological uncertainty of the huge mass of available texts, and their division into a myriad of tongues and not easily legible scripts.

Thus it remains an arduous task, even with the help of all auxiliary documentation, whether archaeological or not, to establish precise relationships between the figurative arts (particularly architecture) and whatever sociological, economic, and political data can be recovered by the widest and most patient research.

The inadequacy of religion alone as a key to interpretation is thus obvious, and it is for this reason that one can justify the fact that an Indian—whether Hindu, Jain, or even Muslim—is and always remains above all an Indian, just as a Japanese—atheist, Christian, Shintoist, or Buddhist—is and remains always a Japanese. Bonds exist that develop from a wider cultural fabric transcending religion and manifesting itself in infinitely diverse ways: from structures of logic to ways of expression and communication, to examples of coherent and tangible collective thought, easily defined as the mode of Asian thought but in reality various and elusive, even though offering, from one civilization to another, common essential lines that are remarkably clear. Obviously, the mode of thought also varies in time both in the religious sector and in other fields, without abrupt turns or revolutions, but still with considerable vitality, except during the phase of benumbed immobility immediately following the decisive impact of the colonialist West. Architecture reflects these variations to some extent, since even in Asia it is the principal interpreter of a complex reality in which, however, fixed and more or less undivided points stand out.

The relation between man and nature, resolved in various forms to the disadvantage of man, who is seen as a fragile creature incapable of opposing the violence of natural forces, almost always takes the form of an artificial symbolism that alludes to the extinction of the human being within the very essence of the universe. A geocentric vision, theories concerning a multiplicity of magical centers (which also have an effect on the form and location of sacred monuments), an indifference toward the individual and the resulting supremacy of the universal and absolute over the individual ego, the greater importance attached to the concept of space as compared to that of time—all these are common Asian elements that have had considerable repercussions in the sphere of the figurative arts, including architecture. Clear-cut and linear in the Far East, hyperplastic in India and in Indianized areas (where it is always connected with sculpture), Asian architecture elaborates an infinity of types different from those of the West, and which at times correspond to exclusively Asian needs. We might mention "umbrella and sunshade" architecture, to use Le Corbusier's expression for his planning at Chandigarh, extending it beyond India to a vast Far Eastern area.

We can also speak of life as it is lived at ground-level, since in many countries (particularly Japan) human existence in the house is conditioned by the Eastern manner of sitting, and does not observe the Western system for household living. Thus, the floor is not only a surface to be walked on, but a welcoming support, neat and polished, while the furnishings are kept low. Elsewhere—in Muslim Asia, for example—we find cushions and rugs as a distant memory of life in tents. We may also recall the *ratha*, the Indian temple in the form of a chariot that merges the choreography of large processional carts with the values of architecture. The relatively illogical principle of its design freezes in stone the slow motion of the carts themselves, filling them with devotional significance and with sexual symbolism as a lesson in life (the classic example is the Temple of the Sun at Konarak, which represents the chariot of the sun god Surya). But the relation between the characteristic social structures of Asia and its architectural types emerges from other examples.

The huge fortresses referred to as "villages with inhabited walls" correspond to the nomadic shepherds' need for security while they were in the process of becoming settled. Their dwellings and storerooms were built into the enormous thickness of the walls (some eighty feet), while the inner rectangle remained free to shelter herds and flocks. Functional in their way, these structures had a combined significance—as an enclosure for animals, as a village, and as a fortified dwelling place for the group. From a socio-economic crisis that involved restricted populations and from the conflict between two hostile worlds (the nomadic and the settled), there emerged shortly before the middle of the first millennium B.C. a complex, organic, architectural structure that cannot be matched elsewhere. Similarly, the Potala at Lhasa and the "castle" at Leh, both in Tibet, are constructions of multiple significance. The nine stories refer to cosmological fantasies, and aside from their symbolism, they represent a combination of palace, fortress, and holy place (they contained, among other things, numerous temples and chapels). Fruits of a society that one might call theocratic—if Buddhism can be said to admit the concept of God as conceived in the West—the two Tibetan complexes combine the sum of religious, political, military, magical, and ecclesiastical values. We refer, of course, to the organizational and hierarchical values of a religious elite.

The architectural phenomenology of Asia thus cannot be compared, under certain aspects, with that of any other civilization. In the hierarchy of the arts, before full contact with the West occurred, architecture was considered by all Asian civilizations to be at an inferior level, since it could be executed immediately and individually. Its use of heavy construction materials, even when the material was wood, required the solution of static and therefore technical problems, as well as the employment of a great number of skilled workers. Even if architecture interpreted the needs of a fixed society and satisfied the taste of that group, it was not held to be capable of the same immediate expression as painting and sculpture. This attitude led to a frequent recourse to symbolism that could easily be understood and appreciated by broad levels of the population.

As a consequence of this approach, the architectural work came to be evaluated and understood primarily in terms of its symbolism. Among all the sources of symbolic inspiration, India is undoubtedly the greatest, not only because she elaborates different forms of symbolism, but also because her religious thought has set up wide-ranging currents that impinge on various local impulses, which thus meet and adapt to one another. Other sources of symbolic inspiration can be singled out—besides those from archaic cultures—in the Iranian and Central Asian area and in the Far East. The predominant motif among them all is the representation of the totality of space and thus of the cosmos.

Such a representation may be unified, as in certain Buddhist stupas, or divided, as in the Temple of Heaven in Peking, where the three-tiered sacrificial area (with nine steps leading up to it to represent the nine levels of Heaven) is completed by a pavilion to the divinity, along with other symbols from Chinese cosmography. The square plan of the other constructions standing before the temple and of certain architectural elements, taken together or as details, allude to the shape of the earth (in Chinese cosmology, the earth is square and the sky round).

The motifs of the world axis and the center of the universe frequently recur in Asian architecture, modulated in various forms according to the period and to particular religious trends. The symbolic Indian source (which is, in its turn, made up of distinct parts but unified by a profound reworking of external influences) remains dominant in every case.

While always primarily inspired by India, Asian architecture in general displays two different modes of construction. With relation to the Asian problem, it is customary to use the word "constructed" for any work in stone, wood, brick, or other material that is built to resolve static and technical problems similar to those revealed in works created by other civilizations. We can by this means distinguish it from architecture that is "cut" into the rock, in which all static problems are resolved by the cohesion of the rock itself. The term "open-air architecture" is not exact, since works cut into the rock exist that are in every way analogous to those that are "constructed"—that is to say, provided with outer and inner space. Nevertheless, rock-cut architecture is found primarily in caves, and in such cases is devoid of outside space. Furthermore, the façades (with or without verandas) have the single purpose of marking and framing in a pleasing manner the openings (for entrance and illumination) necessary for the utilization of these constructions, whose inner space tends to connect the sacred with the essence of the earth.

All cut architecture, however, is a form of pseudo-architecture. While lacking static problems, it uses pillars, ribs, posts, moldings, and spires—the presence of which allude to similar elements in constructed architecture, though they lack any functional purpose beyond the symbolic one. Agreeable to Asian taste and techniques, this type of architecture was extended even to the interior of China. The collaboration between architect, sculptor, and painter is all too evident, to the extent that in the caves of Central Asia, where the petrographic structure of the rock (flaking, crumbling, sliding) prevents careful work, the assistance of the painter or sculptor modeling the divine images in stucco or in plaster on rocky outcrops becomes indispensable and predominant. As for the paintings that adorn the interiors of the cave temples, whether in India or Central Asia, they reveal above all the unconscious desire to dispel the heaviness of the massive, gloomy, encumbering material, which is made even more so by scant illumination. This wish to open windows onto an edifying world that has something of the fabulous can be seen as constant. It was destined to end by exhausting itself in the "tapestry" wall paintings of Tunhwang (at the Central Asian border where the properly Chinese area begins), which, together with the ceiling decorations, have the clear purpose of concealing the walls and the surface of the rock.

If there exist architectural works devoid of external space, there are also typical constructions that lack interior space, and which are therefore similar to giant sculptures. In particular, the Buddhist or Jainist stupa often has no internal space, even though its characteristic symbolism suggests different forms. It may stand for a representation of the whole universe (seen, so to speak, from the outside); it is then formed by a supporting body and a hemispherical or bell-shaped cupola that simply alludes to the celestial hemisphere hanging over the earth, which in Buddhist and Indian cosmology is discoidal; or it may allude to the cosmic mountain, the axis of the universe, sometimes being completed by other symbolic elements that refer to the upward surge of the heavens.

In this second case, the derivation from the Mesopotamian ziggurat is obvious, especially in the stupa with superimposed terraces that imitate a similar meaning in a different form. Sometimes stupas of this type reach gigantic dimensions, like the Borobudur in Java, which is an entire hill transformed into a Buddhist symbol. In India, the form of the stupa tends to be modified by a vertical thrust that depends on taste, and perhaps on the social environment of the particular area. Thus, the so-called stupa of Kanishka—of which only the foundation remains—bore witness to the pride and devotion of the sovereign. Its wooden superstructure reached a height of almost 640 feet, according to later accounts by Chinese pilgrims. It was the magical center of an immense empire in which paranormal powers undoubtedly played a significant part, and was thought to be the highest tower in all of India.

This verticality had conspicuous echoes primarily in China, where the pagoda with its tower was nothing but the transformation of the vertical stupa into an architectural structure provided with organic interior space, thus resuming the same symbols and modifying only their proportions and importance.

Wooden architecture, which prevailed in the Far East, became remarkably widespread in other areas. Apart from the western regions of Central Asia, where whole palaces—Pjanzikent in Sogdiana, for example—were built of wood and survive only as charred remains from the fires that destroyed them, the entire early phase of Indian architecture reveals its unmistakable derivation from wooden prototypes. Not only do stone structures display joints derived from wooden ones, but sculptured ornamental motifs take the place of fastening quoins or of (clearly enlarged) metal nails. Usually we find floral rosette motifs, or, less often, narrative bas-reliefs enclosed in circles, which are interesting for their solutions of compositional and perspectival problems in fully exploiting a circular space. It has been thought that the use of wooden architecture in India and Iran was derived from the Indo-European building tradition. The transition to stone would have taken place at different times in the two countries and for somewhat different, if similar, reasons. In India it occurred late, in part under Iranian influence (the isolated pillars of Asoka), and in part as the manifestation of a liking for cut architecture. Constructed architecture emerged on the basis of the experience accumulated in the use of perishable materials. Its decoration is sometimes created by techniques characteristic of the working of materials other than stone—for example, the collaboration offered by the guild of ivory workers in erecting one of the stupas at Sanchi—and with the purpose of fixing sacred and edifying values in lasting structures. In Iran, on the other hand, stone architecture had a ceremonial and choreographic significance, gave ample development to interior space by exploiting the use of wooden horizontal beams, and exalted the power and regal functions of the ruler.

Stone, worked and employed in accordance with all the experience acquired throughout the ancient Near East (including the territory of the Greeks in Asia Minor), tended to give solidity and permanence to the center of an ecumenical empire that was the religious and magical point of reference as well as a political and administrative seat. Around the large stone constructions, conceived for ceremonial purposes, the dwelling sections remained chiefly in wood. Here the old Indo-European tradition took its place, without disappearing entirely, beside the experiments re-elaborated by a different world, to whose physical aspect contributions had been made by Indo-European groups arriving in the area conquered by the empire in previous periods. It is obvious that the tradition of wooden architecture persisted tenaciously for a number of different reasons, and that the economic factor was not the most important. In the Indian world, on the other hand, the superimposition of Indo-Europeans on Indus civilization produced a social change and a halt in activity that, in the field of technique, brought about a decided regression in the use of brickwork.

But if the Indo-European tradition is linked to wooden constructions, the wooden architecture of Asia is obviously not entirely Indo-European. The ecological structure of the continent suggests the use of wood as the primary construction material. In certain civilizations, such as those of Central Asia, China, and Japan, it preserves its preeminence; in India and Iran, it recedes in the face of brick and stone, despite intermediate phases, as shown by mixed structures (wooden planking in the stupa of Kanishka) and by such examples of coexistence as the capital cities of Iran.

Conclusion

The Asian world, in the broad outlines of its social structure, manifests itself as a complex of highly evolved civilizations in which political power is unlimited and tends to become oppressive, selfpreserving, and thus traditionalist, independent of the aspirations and sentiments of the ruler or rulers holding power. With the exception of those areas where the nomadic cultures and mercantile civilizations of Central Asia developed, the Asian economy is an agricultural one; the city plays a secondary role, while private wealth, mercantile or otherwise, does not confer political power. The subjected masses, whatever their class, have no political choice and cannot overthrow the system under which they live, being at best capable only of changing their rulers.

This lack of choice on the political level is, however, accompanied by considerable freedom on the religious one. This does not exclude traditionalist, habitual, or superstitious ties; what counts in the final analysis is simply one's own convictions and conscience. The paths that lead to the truth are infinite and equally valid. From this arises the prestige and universal value of the religious art work—in particular of the architectural work, which is the sum of esoteric and exoteric wisdom and the precise testimony of a proclaimed truth.

Asian thought, open to every kind of research and speculation, never denies mystical, paranormal, or meditative experiences. Even China—which transforms the essential lines of its own political system into something religiously intangible, reducing the defense of the system to a conflict between *fas et nefas* and neglecting to develop a law, an *ius*, formulated to uphold individual freedom—welcomes such great mystical and meditative trends as, for example, Taoism and Ch'an Buddhism, which expand human consciousness to dimensions beyond the normal ones. There exist thus certain fundamental attitudes of Asian man that—being shared—allow us to consider the whole continent as a unit, a coherent ensemble, made dynamic by economic, political, and cultural phenomena.

In these areas, it is easy to trace the speed of transmission and the extent of expansion of religious ideas, as well as the influences and superimpositions (more or less justified) that manifest themselves with extreme frequency in the sphere of religious thought, but the contacts and borrowings in the other fields are proportionately rarer and less active. Though the Asian architect is never a philosopher or scientist, his creations almost always mirror some religious and philosophical speculation; its essence is grasped by the artist's creative inspiration and aesthetic sense, becoming fixed in forms and examples that in their turn may influence the further development of religious thought. The latter is also a vision of the world, though it usually ignores certain particular aspects and problems of individual and social life, which are considered illusory and thus negligible. In the religious sphere, the individual is virtually free, for persecution is rare, but the development of religious thought unfolds in competition among the various trends. Each of them, therefore, is obliged to undertake activity that we might define as suggestive edification (occult persuasion based on symbolism), and which prompts it to attempt a total detachment of the metaphysical and religious world from the reality of daily social life. Asia also stands in this conflict between two equally pressing realities—the mystical one of divine experience and the sensory one of everyday life. This does not detract, as we have said, from the fact that no opposition whatever exists between the sacred and profane; the religious reality transcends and pervades the existential one, to form a unity with components that only the most recent criticism has begun to analyze with any precision.

These are the undivided foundations that justify the assumption of this book, which is the treatment in a single volume of the architectural works produced by very different civilizations, capable of expressing themselves in styles and forms quite remote from each other, but always united against a common background that we can only define as Asian. As for the sequence and variation of such styles and forms, it will be the task of the individual authors to present their phenomenology and development. I hope merely to have sketched, if only in broad outlines, the unifying characteristics of Asian civilization as they relate to architecture.

Mario Bussagli

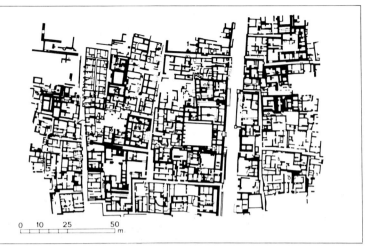

0 10 25 50 m.

1. *Mohenjo-Daro (Pakistan), plan of the city (from Volwahsen, 1969).*
2. *Mohenjo-Daro, view of the Great Bath.*
3. *Mohenjo-Daro, remains of constructions and drainage canal.*

At the beginning, in the third millennium B.C., the most important aspect of Indian architecture was centered on urban planning. It is apparent that the problems that arose were faced and resolved by avant-garde solutions unique for so remote a period. In a context of rigidly planned, standardized structures and works, two great metropolises, Mohenjo-Daro and the city known to us as Harappa, reveal the prevalent city-planning interests of their unknown architects. What counts is the city itself—in its entirety, in its perfect correspondence to an incredibly modern rationalism, in its simple presence. Monuments in the true sense, whether sacred or profane, are lacking, and the search for variations in taste and conception of individual architectural works is slight. Planned, functional, with its dwelling units made uniform according to the social class of the inhabitants, constructed of baked bricks but with an ample use of wood for superelevations, Mohenjo-Daro—India's most ancient city—takes its place in a vast phenomenon of urbanization extending in isolated spots over an enormous territory.

At the same time, large cities were emerging in Turkmenistan (Namazza-tepe and other centers on the Tedzent River), and in Afghanistan (Mundigak and Shahr-i-Sokhta on the Hilmand River), but the economies sustaining them were very different from and less complex than the system that produced urbanization in the Indus basin. The activity of these proto-civilizations was remarkable, so much so that the influence of the Afghan cities of the Hilmand reached the eastern shores of the Arabian peninsula. It cannot be compared, however, to that of Indus civilization. The difference in level is shown by the lesser rationality of the urban structure (which was sometimes grandiose), by more restricted economic specialization, and by the absence of writing. However, the Turkmeno-Afghan phenomenon—whose physical aspect we now know with some precision as a result of very recent discoveries—also sheds light on the genesis of the proto-Indian civilization of the Indus.

After a preparatory phase (improperly called pre-urban) characteristic of the archaic center of Kot Diji and other lesser ones, the Indus basin saw the almost sudden emergence—in the first half of the third millennium—of a splendid civilization, whose territory was the vastest among ancient civilizations. City planning reached extraordinary levels of activity and rationality. The metropolises were laid out on a grid plan (the sign of precise and rigorously maintained planning) and there is every indication of a division into neighborhoods in accordance with the productive specialization of the inhabitants, along with a highly modern interpretation of the distance between home and place of work. The project bespeaks a hierarchical social structure, which seems to be confirmed by the presence of fortified citadels with huge walls, erected on an artificial elevated base. The citadel, in fact, may have been the seat of a strongly oppressive oligarchical power, besides being a secure refuge during invasions (which were unlikely and are in any case undocumented) and during the frequent floods. Strict rationalism is shown by the installation of public utilities—

caravan resting places at the large street crossings, grain silos with openings at the top, public baths that may have had a sacred character, drainage canals and sewage systems. It is possible that the physical orientation of the city was in accordance with the prevailing winds, so as to ensure occasional cleaning of the streets by natural means.

The civilization of the Indus Valley declined because of a profound ecological change produced by its own expansion and activity. The colossal demand for baked bricks and construction lumber brought about extensive deforestation in the entire basin. This in turn led to more frequent and destructive floods, a threat that increased with subsequent changes in the incline of the river bed, altered as well by slow coastal earth tremors. The energy and activity of the bearers of this civilization, predominantly proto-Dravidians, are evident in their capacity to reconstruct immediately those cities destroyed by the river. Mohenjo-Daro, for example, was rebuilt at least seven times. Nevertheless, these ancient builders were caught in a vicious circle of which they were unaware, and by their very capacity to respond promptly to the violence of nature, ended by increasing this violence themselves. With their energies exhausted, the civilization they had created declined and ultimately disappeared (the Aryan invasion about the middle of the second millennium B.C. was also a contributing factor).

The economic structure—based on intensive agriculture, on the cultivation of flax and cotton, on exports and trade (by land and sea) over a wide area—permitted the accumulation of great wealth. Nevertheless, there are no traces of temples, nor of the pomp that usually accompanies royal courts. The complex religiosity of the peoples of the Indus excluded the use of large sacred images, and must very likely have caused them to turn more to psychically evocative forms and to orgiastic rites than to concrete representations.

The concept of the city, with the exception of its public bath and the so-called palace of Mohenjo-Daro (which—approximately 240 by 82 feet—was one of its large, functional, but not rich buildings), was formulated according to a collectivist utilitarianism and a planned functionalism. In all likelihood, these two factors subordinated any aesthetic considerations to the prevailing requirements of the urban system. All the houses, some of which had more than one story, had central courtyards on which the doors and windows opened. Entrance doors were placed on the lesser side streets. As a result, the principal streets, which were not wide, were lined by walls that were uninterrupted except by cross streets; there were no recesses or openings of any other kind. Thus the architectural work was the city itself, not the temple, which did not exist or was replaced by the public baths. Neither was it the palace, which was of such remarkable size but nevertheless does not exhibit the magnificence of this vanished world.

Of the proto-Indian phase, also characterizing the now-buried dry docks of the port of Lothal, not much survives. The collision with Indo-European civilization, which violently superimposed itself on that of the Indus,

17

6. *Patna (Pataliputra), column from the palace of Asoka.*

7. *Lauriya Nandangarh, commemorative column of Asoka with inscription and seated lion.*

8. *Fortress of Allahabad, commemorative column of Asoka (originally from Kausambi).*

9. *Capital with lions from column of Asoka (Sarnath, Museum).*

10. *New Delhi, Kotila-i-Firuz Sah, column of Asoka (stamba).*

probably gave rise to intermediate and restricted forms of culture, but only at the level of the village or small town. Such forms, however, are dubious and had no results, since the Indo-European architectural tradition was founded on construction in wood. The walls of Rajagriha (modern Rajgir), an ancient semilegendary capital, are the only architectural vestiges that remain of a long period extending until the invasion of Alexander the Great into northern India and the founding of the first national Indian Empire, the Maurya dynasty. Creative effort at that time was directed only to poetry and religious thought, which explains why the period in question is generically called Vedic. The large collections of sacred hymns called the *Vedas*, together with a respectable body of texts of another kind, formed the basis of this Brahmanic culture.

Construction was in wood and, given the characteristic climate of the subcontinent, wood could not last for long, not even in such areas more favorable to its preservation as those of the mountainous arc in the north. The preservation of wooden architecture in some regions—in Kashmir, Nepal, and Bhutan—does, however, arouse one's interest in the techniques and forms employed. Elsewhere, the difficulty of providing for a sufficient quantity of suitable lumber, the further threat to its preservation caused by various animal species (especially insects), and the wish to create durable works worthy of religious prestige—all reduced wooden architecture drastically. Naturally, we have no way of determining how the total disappearance of possible, and even imposing, wooden constructions may have altered the evidence now available to us. Suffice it to recall, in this

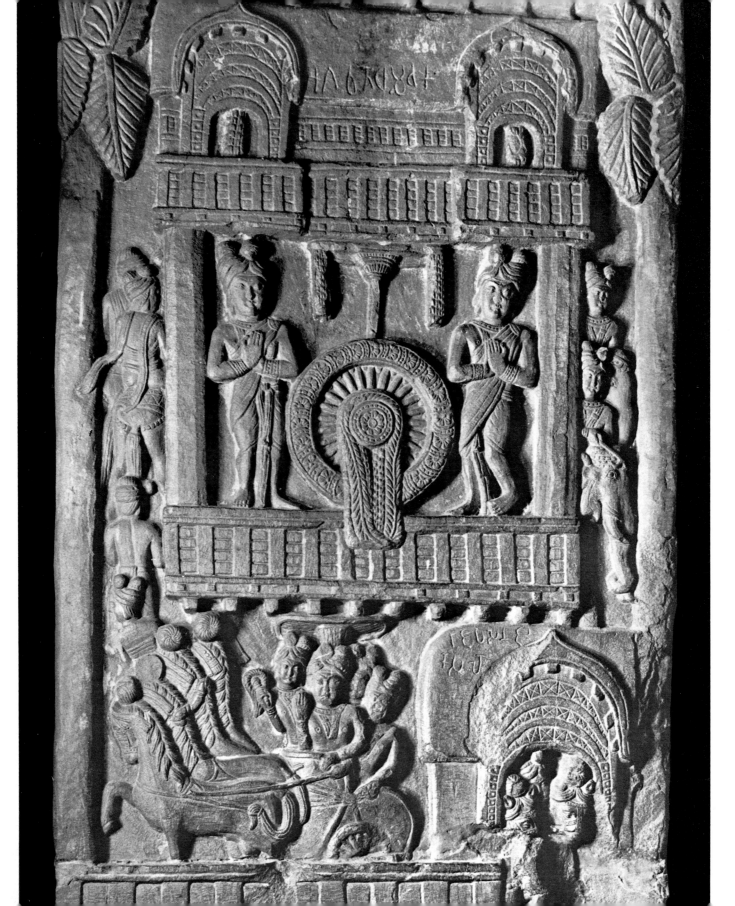

connection, that the wooden superstructure of the so-called stupa of Kanishka at Shah-jiki-Dheri (near Peshawar) carried it to a height of 638 feet, more than doubling the height of the masonry structure; only the rectangular foundations remain today. If the stupa had not been celebrated for various reasons, and if Chinese texts had not spoken of it as the "highest tower" in all of India, we surely could not have imagined the importance of its integration of materials.

The prevalent use of wood has caused a considerable gap in the history of architecture, extending over a period of time that greatly exceeds half a millennium. The only available evidence we have that is worthy of attention begins to come to light in the Maurya period, when the subcontinent was practically unified from the political standpoint and was strongly pervaded by Buddhist thought, which Asoka—the last of the great Maurya rulers—tended to transform into a political ideology. Open to wide contacts with different worlds as a result of Alexander's expedition and the influx of refugees loyal to the defeated Persian Empire, in contact and conflict with the Greek world created by Alexander's successors, India reached a truly significant turning point. In the area of construction materials, we find the first documented use of stone by means of a technique that was derived in part from foreign influences, and in part by imitating techniques used for other materials or discovering them anew. As for brick, whether raw or baked, there existed important ancient traditions that had been only partially lost.

First of all, in the Maurya phase, we find the appearance of stambas, isolated pillars topped by a capital supporting symbolic animal or inanimate figures; their function is primarily magical and religious. They are, in fact, symbols of the "center," in that they indicate the point of convergence—and hence of irradiation—of paranormal forces that, spreading outward, uphold a particular religious persuasion. It is more likely that they were erected by Asoka and not, as some scholars believe, by his father and predecessor, Bindusara. They were, in practice, Persian construction elements used in a different way. By losing their static function as supports, they became true symbols yet preserved their entire original appearance, including the characteristic bell-shaped capital (called Persepolitan), which culminates, however, in the final esoteric sign. From this capital, the use of which became very widespread even in plastic decoration and edifying narrative sculpture, the round amalaka (or cushion-shaped) capital characteristic of later Indian architecture was eventually derived. The form would also be used as the outer termination of the cupolas of temples, likewise designated as amalaka.

Rock-Cut Architecture

The first dated evidence of rock-cut architecture goes back to the Maurya period. In the Indian world, it is necessary to distinguish, over a long period of time, between truly constructed architecture (improperly called open-air architecture, as mentioned in the Introduction) and the kind that is cut into

the rock, frequently inside caves in homogeneous rocky embankments where there is a sheer cliff. This type of construction is typical of India. Rock-cut architecture emerged as a result of the rapport that Indians almost instinctively feel to exist between the sacred sphere and the bowels of the earth. It later spread over a considerable part of Asia, following the extension of Buddhism outside India (the sacred home of Buddhism), though with certain variations in technique and interpretation. We may consider it a traditional religious element, linked to the diffusion of Indian taste and to a particular persistence of its symbolic values, which at times undergo the effects of adaptation to cultural environments highly different from their original one.

Rock-cut architecture is always of a particular kind, one in which all static problems are automatically resolved by the cohesion of the rock itself. Since constructions in caves are endowed exclusively with interior space and only a bare suggestion of a façade that may or may not have a veranda, it is easy to observe in them elements that—though devoid of any static importance—tend to preserve the appearance of the interiors of constructed works. Their presence reveals the concern of the builders to respect a taste (and a symbolism) that by that time had become traditional. If static problems do not exist in works of this kind, there obviously exist others, deriving from the technique for excavating the rock[1] (based on the use of chisels and iron wedges of various sizes and on the creation of parallel excavation galleries) to the effects of light and shadow produced by the scant penetration of light from the outside. On the other hand, the technique of cut architecture was extended with the passage of time to virtually monolithic constructions endowed with both interior and exterior space. It is a sort of sculptured architecture, suggested in part by the hyperplastic character of Indian architectural taste, and evidenced by such famous works as the celebrated temple of Kailasanath at Ellora erected by the Rashtrakuta dynasty between the middle of the seventh and the middle of the eighth century A.D. or the stupendous chapel near Kalugumalai, dedicated to Siva by the Pandya rulers of southern India.

Outside Indian territory proper—in the Khulm Valley in Afghanistan—we find a rather ancient example of cut architecture, one that dates back to the fourth or fifth century A.D. This is the stupa and adjoining monastery of Haibak, known to the ancients as Samangan or Simingan. The monastery, cut inside a cave, is characterized by an unusual plan whose function is exceptional and symbolic, with small half-columns topped by Ionic half-capitals. These represent the translation into rock of particular static solutions that pertain to Sassanian Iran, adopted to support the cupolas overhanging square rooms. But the most interesting monument of the Haibak complex is the stupa. This is the term for a certain kind of construction with a full cupola and rich in symbolic values, used both by Buddhists and Jains. Here at Haibak the cupola, or rather pseudo-cupola, representing the celestial vault as observed from the outside, is monolithic

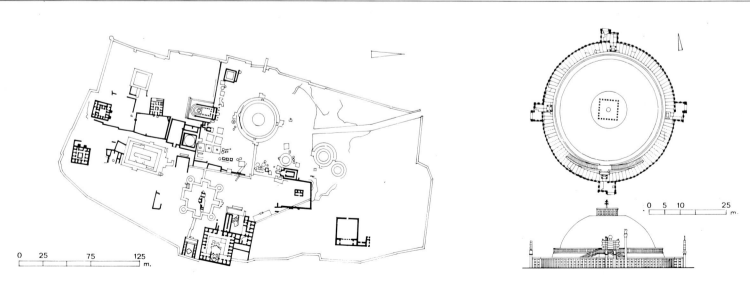

and full as usual. Unlike constructed cupolas, however, it could not accommodate in its interior what is called the foundation deposit, the necessary and consecrating element of every Buddhist stupa, always connected with the "body" and word of Buddha.

The Haibak construction, which required strenuous economic and technical efforts, as well as an enormous amount of labor, was not perfectly orthodox. Moreover, if it is true that the trench that was dug to isolate the form of the cupola was supposed to be filled with water,[2] the stupa would have represented the terrestrial disk surrounded by the ocean. In this case, even symbolically, the stupa at Haibak would not have been entirely traditional, since its significance, rather than being cosmological, would seem to have been connected with the earth and ocean. The *harmika* (the balcony over the cupola, which here has a cell) represented the point of intersection between the human and the divine, thus making concrete a concept widely developed in Mesopotamian ziggurats. Surrounded by a ring of water and partially visible in the reflection, the stupa at Haibak must have represented a true *unicum*. Symbolism aside, the exceptional character of the work is important to us in that it shows that both methods of rock-cutting had reached beyond the territory of India between the fourth and fifth centuries. It reveals, too, that there existed a desire to create unusual effects—the symbolic and ornamental association with water is almost a kind of liquid architecture—and an interest in the creation of forms deliberately devoid of interior space. There is no need, therefore, to wait for later periods in order to place cave architecture side by side with the rock-cut constructions that have both interior and exterior space.

As for works extracted from caves, the first that we know goes back, as mentioned earlier, to the Maurya period. It is dated by the inscription

22. Sanchi, Great Stupa and view of the eastern gate.
23. Bhaja, Chaitya No. 12, section (from Volwahsen, 1969).
24. Magadha, city gate of Kusinagara; reconstruction from a relief on the southern gate of the Great Stupa at Sanchi (from Volwahsen, 1969).
25. Sanchi, Stupa No. 2.
26. Sanchi, Stupa No. 3.

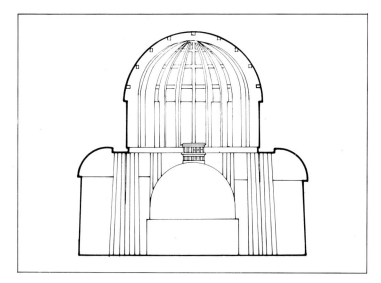

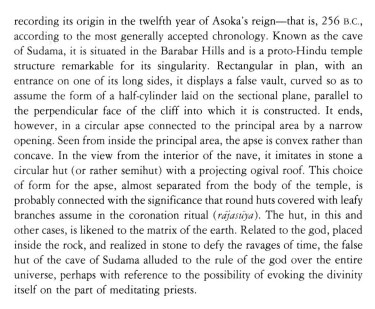

recording its origin in the twelfth year of Asoka's reign—that is, 256 B.C., according to the most generally accepted chronology. Known as the cave of Sudama, it is situated in the Barabar Hills and is a proto-Hindu temple structure remarkable for its singularity. Rectangular in plan, with an entrance on one of its long sides, it displays a false vault, curved so as to assume the form of a half-cylinder laid on the sectional plane, parallel to the perpendicular face of the cliff into which it is constructed. It ends, however, in a circular apse connected to the principal area by a narrow opening. Seen from inside the principal area, the apse is convex rather than concave. In the view from the interior of the nave, it imitates in stone a circular hut (or rather semihut) with a projecting ogival roof. This choice of form for the apse, almost separated from the body of the temple, is probably connected with the significance that round huts covered with leafy branches assume in the coronation ritual (rājasūya). The hut, in this and other cases, is likened to the matrix of the earth. Related to the god, placed inside the rock, and realized in stone to defy the ravages of time, the false hut of the cave of Sudama alluded to the rule of the god over the entire universe, perhaps with reference to the possibility of evoking the divinity itself on the part of meditating priests.

Architecture in Wood and Stone
The most important aspect of the false hut in the cave of Sudama is its demonstration of the profound influence exercised by wooden constructions over those in stone. Here symbolic reasons prompted the imitation in stone of a circular wooden hut. Elsewhere, the interdependence of wooden and

IV. Sarnath, Dhamek stupa.

29. Bedsa, entrance to the chaitya.

30. Bedsa, interior of the chaitya, detail of capitals.

31. *Bedsa, interior of the chaitya.*
32. *Bedsa, interior of the chaitya, scupltured reproduction of the exterior of a house.*

33. *Kondane, rock sanctuary, exterior.*

stone constructions is confirmed by a quantity of secondary data. Thus, the balustrades that define the sacred area around Buddhist stupas—though made of stone—display joints that are absolutely identical with wooden joints, and simulate in their heaviness the balustrades constructed with large logs. With all the irrationality of adopted solutions (requiring much labor and the resolution of considerable technical difficulty), they confirm that the use of stone imitates—for reasons of taste as well—that of analogous constructions in wood. Ornamental rosettes, with or without figures, but in which the motif of the lotus corolla always recurs, are placed at the points of intersection of the upright posts and the crosspieces—precisely at the points where cones and wedges functioning as nails were inserted into wooden constructions. Elsewhere, as for example in the chaityas (or sanctuaries) of Bahja and Karli, wood was actually employed to complete the interior structures of rock-cut constructions. In fact, in the two cases

34. Kanheri, Chaitya No. 3, exterior.

35. Karli, chaitya, elevation of the façade, longitudinal section, ground plan, and detail of a pillar (from Volwahsen, 1969).

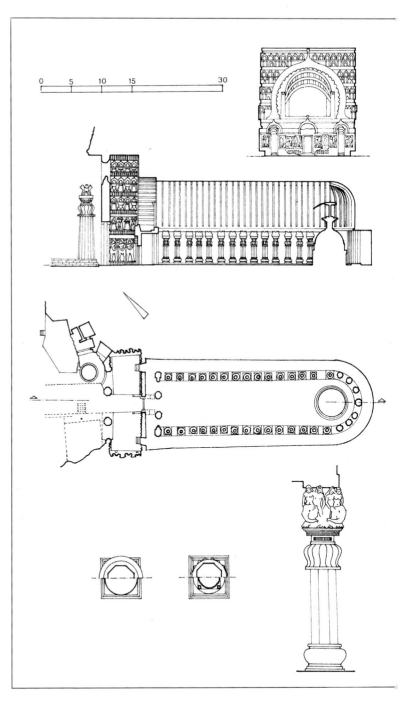

mentioned, the ribs of the vault are of wood; they are thus ornamental elements that allude to methods employed for wooden buildings unknown to us. They indicate, however, the existence of a definite and deep-seated taste that could not be ignored without extreme effort.

The use of such lasting materials as stone and brick is primarily connected with sacred constructions. Moreover, in Buddhist and Hindu India, even if a constant and substantial commitment to lasting works of art did not exist, there was an inevitable tendency toward building in a durable fashion.

Durability and Economics

In non-Indian civilizations, it would seem absurd to detach the architectural work from the concept of durability. Usually, the collapse of a scarcely finished construction, even in regions bordering on India, was due to technical deficiencies and was considered a true calamity. Roman prisoners

36. *Karli, interior of the chaitya, nave with the stupa.*

37. *Nasik,* sangharāma, *exterior of Chaitya No. 18.*

38. *Nasik,* sangharāma, *interior of Chaitya No. 18.*

39. *Udayagiri, caves of Rani Kanaur, exterior.*

40. *Surkh Kotal (Afghanistan), Temple of Fire.*

41. *Haibak (Afghanistan), monolithic stupa, detail of upper part with terrace cell* (harmikā).

42. *Taxila, city walls of Sirkap.*

43. *Taxila, small stupa on the site of Sirkap.*

44. Taxila, Temple of the Double-Headed Eagle on the site of Sirkap.
45. Taxila, distyle in antis temple on the site of Sirkap.
46. Taxila, temple of Jandial.

and the emperor Valens himself (head of the Eastern Roman Empire from 364 to 378 A.D.) were assigned by their Persian captors to the arduous construction of a bridge, Bandi-Kaisar ("Caesar's bridge"), which is still in use. The explicit recognition of Roman technical superiority, even in the midst of a desire to humiliate the conquered foe, was obvious. This superiority translated itself into terms of durability still more than into terms of building science.

In India, especially for the Buddhist population, there existed instead a notably different standard of judgment. If a work was built in order to acquire merit, which was to a greater or lesser extent a constant aspiration, what mattered most was the intention and the sacrifice in money and labor involved in carrying it out. The work, seen as a votive offering, was a gift, a donation of invested wealth and labor. Therefore, even if it collapsed upon completion, it nevertheless had already fulfilled its function. From the economic and technical standpoint, this concept had curious results. Construction frequently brought about only a limited circulation of wealth from the patron to the builders (who were also motivated in part by a desire to acquire merit), since the work created was an end in itself and in theory was not built to last. From the technical point of view, this mental concept ensured that the builders preferred inexpensive, makeshift techniques, quickly applied, and paid only cursory attention to problems of stability. The widespread use of stucco in the northwest can be connected almost always with this desire to build hastily without an excessive concern for a structure's durability.

Naturally, when there was a question of glorifying a site of extreme religious importance, or when the patron attributed a particular value to the work he commissioned, the incentive toward lasting construction, maintenance, restoration, or indeed reconstruction became the rule. Furthermore, durability contributed to the fame of a particular temple or sanctuary. Tradition, reasserting itself, imparted a particular vitality to the architectural complex, resulting in a constant influx of pilgrims and casual visitors—a virtual reflex activity whose importance (economic as well) cannot be denied. In other words, a derivative economic traffic (in votive offerings, souvenirs, temporary facilities for food and lodging, etc.) flourished around the holy centers, involving not only the clergy, but also—and primarily—the groups and individuals attached to this marginal economy. Thus it happened that there emerged around every stupa or temple of some importance temporary dwellings designed to be inhabited by those who lived off the fame of the temple, as well as other constructions suitable for sheltering this traffic. Moreover, the very structure of the huge medieval temples—frequently formed by a group of different constructions contained within a single consecrated rectangular enclosure—was connected with such services as the temple itself required, and with the presence of this marginal but by no means negligible economy that had installed itself outside the enclosure.

47. Taxila, Dharmarajika stupa.
48. Taxila, temple of Kunal.
49. Taxila, remains of a monastery near the temple of Kunal.

50. Stupa from Taxila (Taxila, Museum).
51. Kabul (outskirts), stupa of Guldara.

41

For other reasons, not the least being the limited need for interior space in Hindu temples, the solution of problems of stability was based on an exploitation of gravity that featured building enormous walls, with the entire structure diminishing upward like a pyramid. Form and decoration were often obtained by subsequent cutting and carving. Still, even though a remarkable number of Indian works have survived the ravages of time, the characteristic relativism of Indian thought with respect to the importance given to architectural works (and not only to these, but to all of sensory reality) constitutes a degree of appreciation that is undeniable. However, this appreciation must be viewed beside the characteristic coexistence of constructed and cut architecture, along with the relative implications of works "cut in the negative sense"—that is to say, in caves (with interior space only)—and those "cut in the positive sense" (with exterior space, either with or without interior space). These observations, implying as they do a highly special flexibility in the evaluation of the architectural media, are sufficient to underscore the originality and autonomy of the architectural phenomenon in India.[3]

Aesthetic Value

In the traditional hierarchy of artistic activity, India bestows the highest value on poetry, the theater, dance, painting, and music. Architecture, along with sculpture and the minor arts, was considered almost a craft, even though it required of the architect exceptionally vast knowledge touching on the most diverse fields, including empirical knowledge of a geological sort and

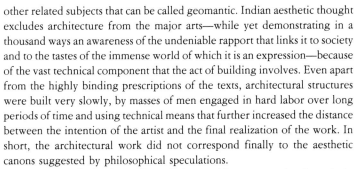

other related subjects that can be called geomantic. Indian aesthetic thought excludes architecture from the major arts—while yet demonstrating in a thousand ways an awareness of the undeniable rapport that links it to society and to the tastes of the immense world of which it is an expression—because of the vast technical component that the act of building involves. Even apart from the highly binding prescriptions of the texts, architectural structures were built very slowly, by masses of men engaged in hard labor over long periods of time and using technical means that further increased the distance between the intention of the artist and the final realization of the work. In short, the architectural work did not correspond finally to the aesthetic canons suggested by philosophical speculations.

There is no doubt that Indian religious architecture, predominant in its importance and abundance, reflects Indian civilization better than any other of its means of artistic expression. That civilization, as we know, leaves the widest possible margin for religious speculation. Apart from the sacred significance attributed to construction materials (whether wood, stone, or brick),[4] Indian architecture obeys a unique—that is to say, a religious and symbolic—"functionalism." The very act of building—which began by determining the rapport between the universe and the chosen terrain, with geomantic appraisals and the exorcising of *bhūtas* (demons and spirits) from the site as well as gods other than those to whom the temple was dedicated—had the value of a magical rite. There was a full awareness of the "sacrifice" of which the earth was victim, withdrawn as it was from cultivation and destined to support the weight of the wall structure. It was

60. Buddh Gaya, temple of the
Mahabodhi.

61. Badami, Rock Temple No. 2,
detail of the entrance.
62. Badami, portico of Rock Temple
No. 1.

thought necessary to placate the earth through the rite of *vastuśamana* in order to establish a favorable relationship between the creative force of the earth itself and the human work that was to rise on it. There existed thus a kind of rapport between architecture and nature, formulated on the basis of invisible forces rather than on those of aesthetic harmony. Now, the magical basis of such rituals, the multiplication and interweaving of symbolic elements, the very fact that the construction of a religious structure could be likened to a liturgical act—all seem to have excluded in the most absolute fashion any urgent search for *rāsa*, a term that refers to the very substance of the aesthetic experience (although it has numerous meanings, the chief one being "flavor"). But if traditional classifications relegated architecture to a secondary plane, the works created were not rendered less valid thereby, as is proved by the universal appreciation accorded them today. Nevertheless, even in the Indian world and despite their negative premises, works of architecture enjoyed a popularity that precluded any complicated reading of the symbolic and religious values they incorporated.

We find traces of this in literary works: temples, independent of their symbolism, are compared in their bulk to huge mountains,[5] but still more significant is the suggestion offered by the *Cūlavamsa*, a Pali-Singhalese work, which in describing the ruins of Polonnaruwa compares them to old men who bend more and more toward the ground with the passage of time. The same text speaks of constructions that, "rising in stone or brick, create a pleasure for the eyes." This clearly corresponds to a particular impression aroused by the work of art outside of its religious and symbolic implications. The critical attitude reflected by the Pali-Singhalese text, like that shown in other works that strive to express the grandeur of certain temples through unexpected or daring metaphors, leads back to one of the most valid and widespread currents of thought.

The aesthetic speculation of Dandin, Sanskrit author and poet of the sixth century, points out in fact that the *rāsa* to which we refer is nothing but a state of mind, a sentiment intensified by a combination of different elements but essentially a normal one (which as a result can be perceived and expressed in the literary forms of which we have spoken), even when it is prompted by forms that turn out to be partially accidental, as in the case of the Polonnaruwa ruins. It is obvious that the exterior decoration—constantly hyperplastic due to the inseparable relation between architecture and sculpture—has an influence on the impressionistic value aroused by the enormous size of religious architectural structures. Because of such a phenomenon, the symbolic component of the work and the myriad images adorning its exterior intervene almost unconsciously; they blend into a single significance that is generally connected with the mountain, with its upward thrust, and with a vision that reunites the concretions of the earth—that is to say, mountains—with a spiritual effort at elevation. The direction of the effort is toward achieving a reality that precludes all that is relative or contingent.

65. *Aihole, temple of Lad Khan, exterior.*

66. *Aihole, temple of Durga, detail of sculptured decoration of a pillar.*

67. *Aihole, temple of Durga, exterior of apse.*

68. *Aihole, temple of Durga, exterior.*

69. *Aihole, city walls.*
70. *Sanchi, Monastery No. 45.*
71. *Sanchi, Temple No. 18.*

72. *Kanchipuram, temple of Kailasanath; in the foreground, the mandapa.*

73. *Mamallapuram, Dharmaraja* rath *(monolithic chariot-temple), elevation, section, aerial view, and ground plan (from Volwahsen, 1969).*

V. Buddh Gaya, temple of the Mahabodhi.

From the Western viewpoint—and limited to sacred Hindu buildings—the effect of the massive temples could be said to have been close to the Baroque in some respects, especially in the movement of surfaces and the resulting play of light and shadow. It was admittedly a swollen, heavy, and exotic Baroque, but rich in effects and rendered abstruse by the diversity of its artistic language and expressive means. Indeed, the decoration and the treatment itself of the images obeyed a foreign and vexing taste when measured against Western choices and experience. Nevertheless, it was precisely because of this similarity, superficial and poorly understood though it was, that even the Indian experience helped (indirectly) in the paradoxical definition of the Baroque as a "category of the human spirit," at a particular moment when critical thought was directed at this artistic trend.

In reality, the architecture of India can be evaluated only on the basis of the culture that produced it, it being understood that it offers universal values, suggestions, and sentiments no different from those recorded in Indian literature. The degree and intensity of these impressive appraisals are obviously modified as a result of the modes of thought and fixed hierarchies of values corresponding to the diversity of those cultures that from time to time have confronted the discovery or the knowledge of Indian architecture. In any case, there is a clear aesthetic difference between Buddhists and Hindus, which can be related to the essence of their respective quests for truth. The search of the Buddhist is directed toward an ideal of peace and serenity; in Hinduism, there is a prevailing dynamism (and a movement of architectural volumes) that attempts to express a divine majesty shining through the very life of the universe. The first philosophy, however linked to cosmic symbolism, is based on a human measure. The second has as its parameter the rhythm of life of the universe; it transcends the individual and his destiny, as well as his range of mental sentiments, to express an overwhelming awe of the sacred.

This is not to deny that the great sacred works of Buddhism and Hinduism are the fruit of a highly particular social situation that concentrates the tremendous efforts of generations therein, to the detriment of other undertakings which the religious spirit (in its way relativistic because lacking in real barriers of orthodoxy) of Indian culture has made to appear less urgent. The drive toward the Absolute, an essential concept of Indian religious speculation, made the reality of social conflict fade. The result has been a lack of interest—not only theoretical—in history and the wish to react to the pressure it exercises upon individuals through a sense of community[6] (Buddhism) and through a hopeless, extremely resigned isolation (Hinduism). Only the certainty of endless reincarnation attenuates the instinctive terror of death, rendering less miserable the life of beings crushed by insuperable, intertwined, oppressive hierarchies. The only full, free, fundamental, and respected choice was that of religious belief. Ideas of this kind were reflected in the field of the figurative arts, and thus also in architecture, producing—along with other profound components—forms

and effects that in other civilizations could not even have been imagined. Created by great if anonymous artists, these forms were in essence *prakrti*—that is to say, nature—not only because they were in harmony with the natural surroundings, but also and above all because they were deeply rooted in civilization, in man, in the Indian world in its entirety. For *prakrti* is, after all, the collective unconscious of the Indian people.

The Dominant Theme

To judge by the quite numerous and systematic treatises, the fundamental motif of Indian architectural constructions is the representation of the center. It is a theme equally valid for architecture and for city planning. Every temple or palace was an *axis mundi*, a sacred center in which the celestial, the terrestrial, and even the infernal worlds met. By extension, this symbolic motif also recurred in the plan of cities, it being understood that in all of India, down to our own day, the essential unit of human agglomeration is the village. Thus, the motif of the center found its place in the theoretical plans of cities, whether these were square in shape (the square being the symbol of the ordered world, the perfection of form and of order); rectangular, with the principal streets inscribing a rhombus; or even more abstract (circular, semicircular, or triangular).

The idea for the round plan may be of foreign origin—perhaps Assyrian, by means of the Parthians—but in every case these geometric figures had their own value and symbolic meaning. The constant significance underlying these various symbols is that of converting the magical forces of the soil—pre-existing or assembled and condensed by preliminary foundation rituals—into a basis of support for human cohabitation and into a form of breath or of life, in unison with the rhythm of the cosmic breath. The search is for a human dimension for cities, in order that men may feel therein the rhythm of the universe, which is likewise achieved through the geometric treatment of the indefinite (but not infinite) space of the urban complex. On the other hand, the concept becomes changed and exaggerated when it is a question of sacred constructions. Here the geometric tendency, since it alludes to a greater intensity of the sacred, is even more evident. The plan of a stupa in various periods will be frankly circular, including its surrounding enclosure; or it may display a circle inscribed in a square, or even series of squares. The plan of the Hindu temple will on the contrary be primarily an enclosed rectangle, though sometimes the sides of the enclosure are segments of reversed ellipses; the disposition of the buildings, which can vary considerably, will sometimes be symbolic and sometimes quincuncial, with one building at each corner and one at the center, thus exploiting the diagonals of the rectangle as axes for the placement of structures in space. In every case, there is an obvious attempt to provide isolated visibility for the principal building, which nevertheless forms part of the total order of symbolic (and thus artificial) space constituted by the whole. In a certain sense, this arrangement endowed the hemispheres of

stupas and the huge masses of medieval temples with a prominence that alluded symbolically to the mountain *par excellence*—the cosmic pillar, the axis of the world, made concrete by its man-made replica.

There is clearly, with respect to sacred monuments, a shade of meaning different from what we find in the Western world. In fact, there exists between the sacred and profane a characteristic dichotomy in location that does not exactly correspond to what occurs in the West, especially insofar as theoretical implications are concerned. Sacred constructions are frequently decentralized with respect to urban agglomerates, when not actually isolated. They may be temple cities (Madura), combined temple and monastery complexes (Ajanta), or—as previously stated—isolated temples that attract to their precincts groups of persons having economic connections with the life of the temple. In all such cases, we are in the presence of "centers" in themselves, whose magnificence forms no part of an urban context, but emerges from the desire for a deliberate and specific encounter with the sacred. As such, these centers were purposely created to be alien to the city, but in a form different from that of the Christian monastery or abbey. The city, in its turn, was seen as a consecrated and functional center, designed to connect the sacred with the daily life of a mass of human beings who availed themselves, as a specific and ready reference point for their spiritual needs, of the religious construction that in theory was always placed at the center (but that in practice might be located differently, even though gravitating directly toward the center). The dichotomy between sacred and profane is here reduced to a different degree of intensity. This same human mass—which is never capable of conferring real autonomy on its own city—knew, in return, that it lived in an urban environment where every detail acted to convert the invisible magical and religious forces into influences that were protective, creative, and responsive to the order and divine law that reigned within its walls.

Thus, we find in the texts that the basic structure—generally a rectangular grid—is overlaid by a street pattern that increases the symbolic values of the urban center. Such insertions also provide solutions that satisfy the demands of traffic relating to the location and function of the city itself. A fortified city might be in the form of a *padma* (lotus blossom), preserving the inner network but enclosing it within a quadrilobate ring of circular, octagonal, or hexagonal bastions whose lobes correspond to the corners of the basic square. Other theoretical plans may call for a greater width of the streets, which were oriented in a particular direction; or situate the buildings—always with the basic network in mind—in such a way as to form a symbolic figure (the swastika, for example). Nevertheless, beyond these theoretical considerations, the social reality of the Indian world has conditioned the growth of its cities, producing spontaneous variations in the basic grid pattern and the symbolic geometrical figures. The grid, rigid and undivided, bound up with a town plan, appears at its clearest only in the metropolises and cities of the Indus Valley culture. Although it is

impossible to reconstruct the successive stages, it is known that from these derive the erudite and speculative plans already to be found in the Vedic phase, but which were to be fully developed in technical writings only much later.

It is certain nevertheless that the division of the space under construction into a network of squares and—subordinately—into triangles emerges from requirements of a religious and symbolic kind. However, the geometric treatment of the available space is very different from what we find in modern architecture, and leads to what we might call a multiple visibility for the work. This is because the work itself, as a result of its symbolic significance and its representation in concrete form of a vertical axis (the magical *axis mundi*), must offer equally valid and total views from all sides, thus being subject to a scheme that is more sculptural than architectural. Even the word "façade" takes on a shade of meaning quite different here from its use in the European world and in some other parts of Asia. The façade is determined by points of access to the interior, whose existence it underlines, but it does not prevail over the lateral or apse views. Its symbolism as the center carries the Indian architectural mass as much as possible toward plastic values.

The Development of Architecture in India

It should be pointed out that—aside from the Vedic altar to be found in every village, and which, in its simplicity, is as charged with symbolism as any of the great architectural works—the architecture of India has obviously experienced oscillations in religious thought. It thus keeps pace with the rise of Buddhism, and is later modified by the affirmation of certain trends in Hinduism and the consolidation of Jainism. Nevertheless, it was Buddhism alone that imparted to India a pre-eminent position in the international sphere. It was the expansion of Buddhism—a clearly Indian religion, though heterodox with respect to its Vedic-Brahmanic-Hindu background—that in fact produced Asian humanism. The spread of properly Hindu thought was more limited and less rich in suggestions capable of development.

Beginning with the Maurya period, or more precisely with the reign of Asoka, the architectural constructions that have come down to us are for the most part Buddhist. However, in addition to stambas (isolated pillars), we also find chaityas (sanctuaries) and viharas (monasteries). Besides the chaitya of Sudama that we have already mentioned, there is that of the Lomas Rishi cave, which also displays an entrance with the characteristic *kūdu* (horseshoe arch) that surmounts and frames the entrance and that was to become one of the most widespread motifs in Indian architecture. Used also for upper windows in other typical constructions, it carries over into its execution in stone (as in the caves at Kanheri and Karli, and the early Ajanta caves) the characteristic traits of the wooden *kūdu*, a proof of its derivation from a wooden architecture that has disappeared. As for civil constructions,

81. Gwalior, temple of Teli-ka-Mandir.

82. Kalugumalai, monolithic Vettuvan Koil temple.

83. Pattadakal, temple of Malikarjuna.

there remain the foundations of Asoka's palace at Pataliputra (now Patna), whose splendor was described by the Greek Megasthenes, Seleucid ambassador to the Maurya court. The royal palace on the ancient site of Sirkap at Taxila most likely belongs to the same period; only its ground plan survives, though other remains testify to the former richness of the site. It is very probable that the palace at Pataliputra, destroyed by fire between the fifth and seventh centuries A.D., was partly laid out according to the plans for Achaemenid palaces, taking its inspiration from a similar concept of royalty.

Later centuries offer a much wider panorama. The stupa, as we have often had occasion to mention, is a construction lacking interior space. As a characteristic sacred building, it assumes very different forms in its Indian development, as well as in its diffusion over all of Buddhist Asia. It has a multiple symbolic significance: as a magical center (the axis of the world); as a representation of the universe, seen from outside; as a tomb, cenotaph, or reliquary; as a reminder of edifying or miraculous events. It can also be built as a votive offering or as a sign of the faith erected on new, vast territory. It replaces the importance of the altar and can be considered an architectural image of the Buddha, whose essence permeates the entire universe. Finally, it can vary greatly in size and form, from miniature replicas a few inches high (but with the same importance) to mountain stupas such as the Borobudur of Java, which is an entire large hill transformed into a symbol.

In the period under consideration, we find a number of famous stupas, ranging from that at Bharhut (whose decoration is an example of a school of sculpture in which independent characteristics are mingled with a desire to avoid the anthropomorphic representation of the Buddha by substituting symbols) to the stupa of Buddh Gaya (a reminder of the Buddha's Enlightenment) and the celebrated group at Sanchi in Madhya Pradesh. Stupas at this time are surrounded by a *vedikā* (fence) with open *toranas* (gates) at the cardinal points consisting of vertical posts with horizontal beams. The stupa itself, cylindrical at the base, rises into a body with a false hemispherical dome called an *anda* (egg) surmounted by a kind of small belvedere, the *harmikā*, at whose center an axis—with a series of parasols often diminishing in diameter—represents both the axis of the universe and Buddha.

The period of construction of the stupas at Sanchi is rather controversial. The most probable date is the second or first century B.C., which is almost certainly the date for the so-called Great Stupa, the focal point of the entire sacred complex situated a few miles outside the city. The presence of one of Asoka's pillars confirms the holy tradition of the site from somewhat earlier periods and may supply some foundation for the emperor's presumed visit to pay homage to a small Buddhist community that had settled in the surrounding hills. But, aside from the considerable sacred significance of the complex, what is important is its intermingling of architectural and

84. Pattadakal, temple of Mallikarjuna.

figurative evidence that can be deduced from the decorations. Here the stupa is truly the image, or rather the epiphany, of the Buddha, of his Law that rules the universe (serving in fact in aniconic representations to express the Buddha's presence), and is moreover a psycho-cosmogram. The form, suggested by the apparent aspect of the vault of the sky, implies in its turn the total presence and intangibility (ascribed to the foundation relics) of the Buddha, who in this way is seen not as a human teacher but as the essence of the universe.

The type of stupa with a hemispherical dome is also found in the Andhra school. For example, we have traces of the foundations of the huge stupa at Amaravati, where the diameter of the sacred area is several hundred yards, as well as the remains of other works of the same kind, though smaller in size, found at Nagarjunakonda, Gummadidirru, Prolu, and Guntupala. The domes, more globular, were grafted onto drum bases much higher than the examples at Sanchi. This data is supplied by reliefs with sculptural representations of local stupas; from these we can also see that the stupa of the Andhra school considerably modifies the appearance of the entrance to the sacred area. The *vedikā* (the openings in the outer fence) were flanked with images of facing lions placed at the tops of the posts, while the outer edge of the raised circular walk surrounding the drum halfway up displayed projecting balconies that faced the gates. On these balconies, side by side and joined at their capitals, five pillars of equal height were erected. Their symbolic significance is unknown, but it is assumed that their practical use was to support oriflammes or banners that had a ritual meaning. The presence of verticalized bands, almost surfaces—alternately carved and empty and thus contributing to effects of light and perspective—modifies the globular mass of the stupa and diminishes its isolation while enclosing the dome, conceived so as to exceed a hemisphere in curvature, in a kind of crown. There is thus a change in style that derives from the cultural conditions of the Andhras and from a state of mind that foreshadows future developments in Indian art, which were to be more balanced and knowledgeable.

In the northwest Indian regions—that is, the area of expansion of the so-called Greco-Buddhist art of Gandhara—the stupa acquires a strong vertical thrust. This thrust is frequently obtained by wooden superstructures that must have included series of terminal parasols, transforming the stupa into a conical trunk that sometimes rose to considerable height. We know of this verticality through models, sometimes very elaborate, or through the small stupas to be found in areas outside the Indian subcontinent (in Afghanistan or Central Asia), which though late are sufficient to indicate the direction taken by the Gandhara stupa. An upward thrust, a mysticism not unlike what we find in the Gothic, characterize these productions of the north, from which derive, by various intermediate stages, the Tibetan chorten, where even the dome is distorted to take on the shape of an inverted pot (the term "pot" serves as a technical one). Lamotte has given us an

accurate listing of Indian tower stupas, almost always some 200 feet in height, to be found primarily in the Gandhara region.[7]

The importance of the Gandhara school is not really limited to stupas, though some of these, as in the Takht-i-Bahi complex, find their place in rather scenographic overall solutions that surely show traces of the Classical and Hellenistic component fundamental to this school. Proceeding from the fortifications of Bactra (today known as Balkh), with their Parthian-style decorations and high embrasures, to such Hellenistically inspired cities as Ai Khanum ("Lady Moon" in Uzbek)—which is situated at a bend of the Amu Darya River and preserves the agora, principal street, citadel, and even a *heroon*—or the complex of Kapisa-Begram, one arrives back on properly Indian soil at Taxila. Here we recall Charsadda and Puskalavati, the Greek Peukelaotis and in some respects the sister city Taxila. In practice, virtually all urbanization in the Gandhara region is Greek in character, based on Hellenistic models that are modified only to the extent that local taste suggests different solutions, as for example in the skyline of the chapels that top off the stupa of Takht-i-Bahi. This is not to deny that Gandhara architecture, though employing round support towers, octagonal motifs even in domes, and other elements of foreign derivation, is essentially an autonomous architecture, primarily "constructed," in which Indian, Classical, Iranian, and perhaps Central Asian elements come together. The temple of Jandial at Taxila, for example, is a distyle *in antis* modified to suit the needs of a fire cult. But the Classical component—smothered in such gigantic works as Surkh Kotal, which nevertheless preserves Greek elements—sometimes comes to the surface again in the plan of sacred complexes (Mohra Moradu, Jaulian, and Loriyan Tangai). Here space is divided into an aligned order that places the principal monument at the center, leaves one wing available for cells and chapels, and reserves the other for the erection of the votive stupas. The vertical thrust, already mentioned, is not only an anti-Classical element, but a search for particular effects, deriving from a conception of space entirely foreign to India and nevertheless clearly Gandharan.

In the development of the stupa, the square or rectangular base on which the cylindrical body of the dome-topped drum is grafted becomes a verticalizing element by means of the steep staircases that ascend to the base of the central body of the stupa itself and that are placed at the four sides. Even when the plan of the base is more involved, becoming cruciform or star-shaped, the conception of the space remains an upward one, in a controlled succession of superimposed and diminishing horizontal planes. There remains the overall conception—multilateral (and indeed capable of being enjoyed from every point), static at the base, but animated in the conical trunk of the upper structure. In practice, it can be made objective through the superimposition of the different forms that strengthen the vertically oriented precision of the imaginary line from which the stupa's constituent forms derive.

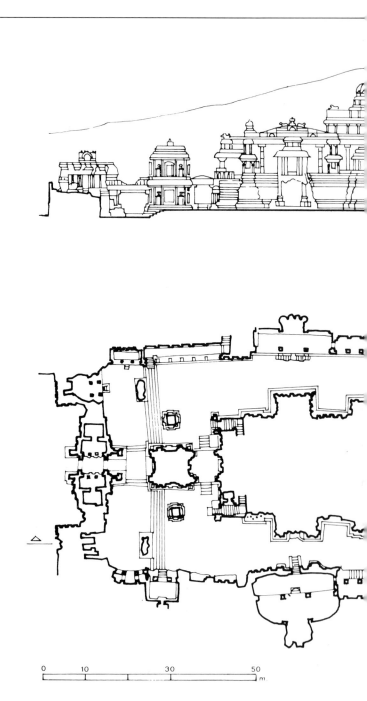

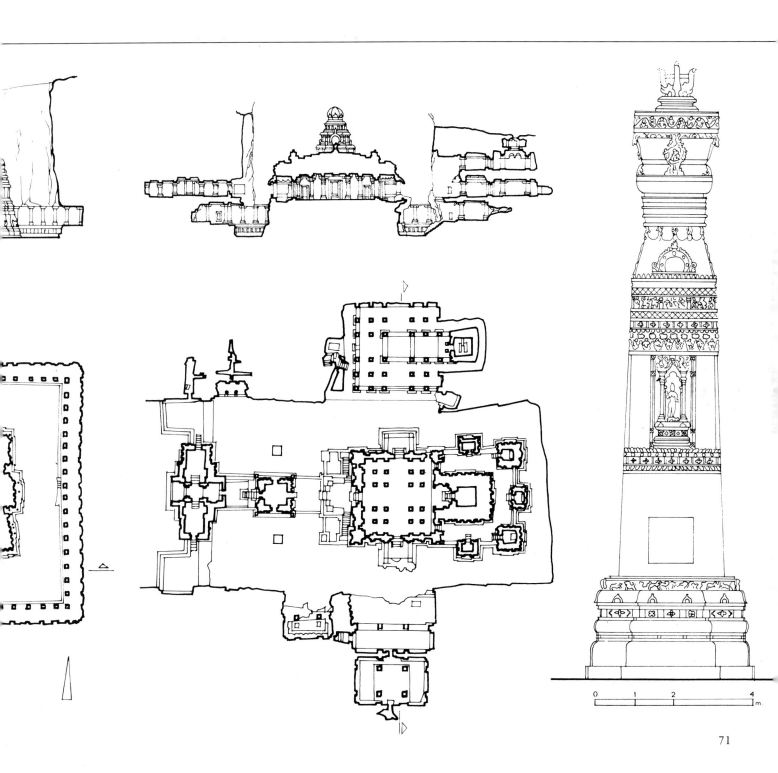

87. Ellora, Kailasanath, elevation,
transverse section, and plans; at the
right, elevation of a monolithic column
in the courtyard of the temple (from
Volwahsen, 1969).

0   1   2   4
m.

88. *Ellora, Kailasanath, detail of the southeast portion.*
89. *Ellora, Kailasanath, exterior.*
90. *Ajanta, view of Caves No. 6-19.*
91. *Ajanta, caves, plan of the complex (from Volwahsen, 1969).*
92. *Ajanta, Cave No. 1, plan.*

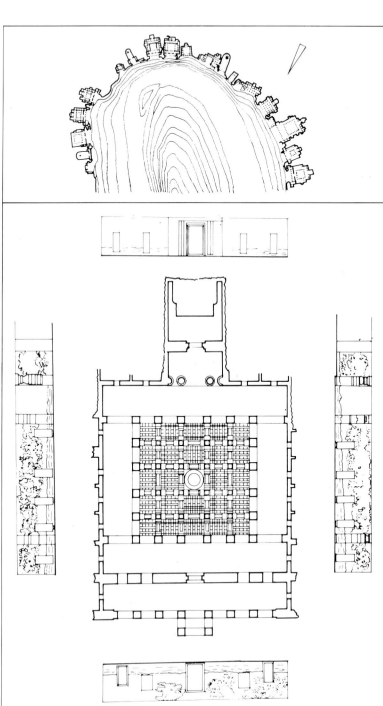

93. *Ajanta, Cave No. 2, plan.*
94. *Ajanta, Cave No. 6, plans of the lower and upper levels.*

95. *Ajanta, Cave No. 9, plan of the chaitya.*
96. *Ajanta, Cave No. 10, plan of the chaitya.*

97. *Ajanta, Cave No. 19, interior of the chaitya, stupa with a representation of Buddha in high relief.*

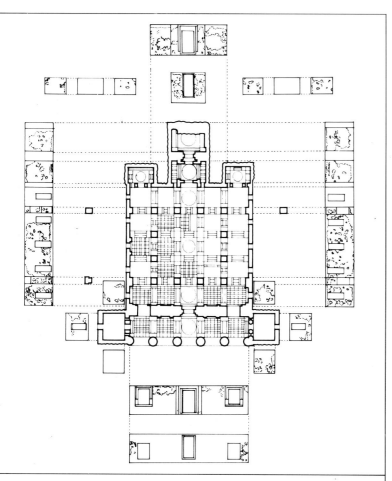

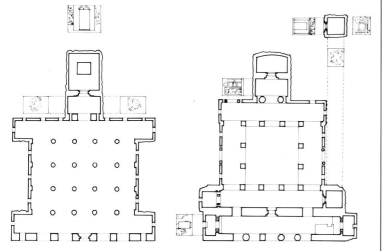

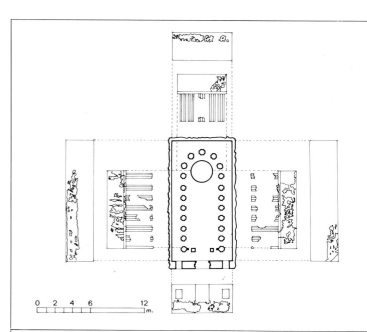

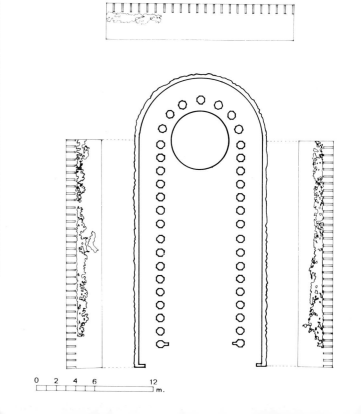

98. *Ajanta, Cave No. 26, interior of the chaitya, stupa with a representation of the seated Buddha.*

99. *Ajanta, Cave No. 26, exterior.*

As for such later stupas as those at Sarnath and Nalanda, one notes an increase in mass and a feeling of heaviness in the constructions. At Sarnath the superimposed cylindrical masses, with collar fittings and greatly flattened terminal ogives, show a structural tension that seems to radiate over the surrounding space. At Nalanda the staircases for access, projecting from the square base so as to form a cruciform plan with a central square, produce effects of geometric and (in a certain sense) of abstract movement that in any case are very far removed from the Indian taste for curvilinear values and soft, rounded forms. As its use spread over Asia, the stupa achieved enormous dimensions, as at Borobudur in central Java during the ninth century; became a commemorative monument, as happened in Central Asia; or lost its character as an architecture without interior space by having a chapel with an image of Buddha installed in the cupola (or rather in the *anda*).

Cave Architecture

The ancient examples from the Maurya period were followed by a considerable range of works hollowed out of the rock, especially of the sanctuaries known as chaityas (though the Sanskrit word is connected with funeral rites of cremation and the ashes of the dead). The chaitya appears to be related to the stupa only by the fact that it contains one in its interior. The plan of the chaitya, of particular interest for its balance and harmony, displays in its final development a particular form, with a semicircular apse and false lateral naves that are too narrow for effective use. At the same time the chaitya becomes elongated. At Bhaja the ratio of width to length, unusually marked by the large central cupola surmounting the stupa, is 1:2.5; at Ajanta, taking into consideration all the chaityas on the site, it can be reckoned at 1:2.7; at Karli it is clearly 1:3. With the passage of time, chaityas thus become larger and more magnificent, approaching, even if remotely, the Western basilica; this means that there was an increasingly broad participation in religious ritual, with a profound change in the social composition of those attending. Moreover, the fact that not only monks but the laity as well participated in rites, exegesis, and the study of doctrine is shown by the large meeting halls for both groups that are already indicated at Bhaja.

Experts all agree in their estimation of the Karli complex as one of the finest artistic achievements of cave architecture—a credible observation, but one that shows how easy it is to perceive the care and application that went into the construction of these works. Similar works, built in the open, influenced those extracted from caves, and this explains why at Karli we find the repetition of an interesting solution for the façade with three entrances, and especially a greater interest in the external space, something already to be seen at Ajanta (Cave No. 19 belonging to the Gupta period).

Sangharāmas (certain monasteries) cut into the rock deserve mention along with chaityas. Their cells had (and have) a quadrilateral plan,

113. Gyaraspur, temple of Mahadevi.

114. Schematic representation of a nāgara temple (from Volwahsen, 1969).

115. Evolution of the plan of a temple from the square form to a polygonal form based on the presumed chronological division of the circle. Example: plan of the holy cell of the temple of Brahmesvara at Bhuvanesvar (from Volwahsen, 1969).

frequently square. They opened onto an inner court—square or rectangular—while a colonnaded veranda ran in front of the cells themselves, shielding them from the sun and allowing persons to pass from one to another under cover; this was also useful during the monsoon season. The *sangharāma* often had two stories, or indeed three. Derived from constructed examples, rock-cut monasteries (requiring a truly enormous expenditure of labor) were almost always more regular. We might mention those of Kondane, Pitalkhora, Nasik, and Karli, as well as Ajanta and the Jain monasteries of Orissa (Khandagiri; Udayagiri). In general, the ceiling of the meeting hall is not sustained by pillars, but in later periods (from the beginning of the full Gupta phase on—that is, from the fifth to the eighth century) the hall becomes hypostyle, while the full development of excavation techniques is shown, so far as *sangharāmas* are concerned, in the two large monasteries of Ellora (eleventh and twelfth centuries). This is an observation, however, that applies primarily to cut decoration, concentrated on pillars and friezes.

Beginning with the Gupta period, while stonecutting techniques improve, there is a growth in the importance and spread of constructed works, which is likewise related to the rebirth and consolidation of Hinduism. The temple of Kailasanath at Ellora, built by Emperor Krishna I of the Rashtrakuta dynasty, is also the fruit of this technical progress. Construction lasted from 756 to 773—that is, during the reign of Krishna I—and the complex, which was slightly larger than the Parthenon in plan and one and a half times as high, was completed down to the last detail in less time than it would have taken to build it in masonry. The construction—or rather, the cutting—proceeded from top to bottom, thus avoiding the need for scaffolding, and the work took shape on the basis of a very detailed plan that was carried out with exceptional care.

A different example, also with regard to the techniques employed (wet wooden quoins), is offered by the seventeen temples of Mamallapuram, of which the one known as the Seven Pagodas preserves archaic Dravidian features. They were cut out of hard granite and are slightly earlier than those works on the island of Elephanta in the harbor of Bombay, which partly echo the style of Ellora and contain the three-headed figure of Siva known as Mahesamurti. These are the last great rock-cut works. From this point on, open-air constructions predominate.

Temples

It is not easy to discern the genesis of the typical and so-called medieval temples of India. There may be an indication of it in a small circular chapel at Bairat near Jaipur that goes back to the third century B.C. It originally contained a stupa, but—except for the foundations—little remains today of this wooden and brick construction. As for the temple of Jandial, of which we have already spoken, it too represents a fixed point in temple construction. The Classical influence it shows, despite the obvious adapta-

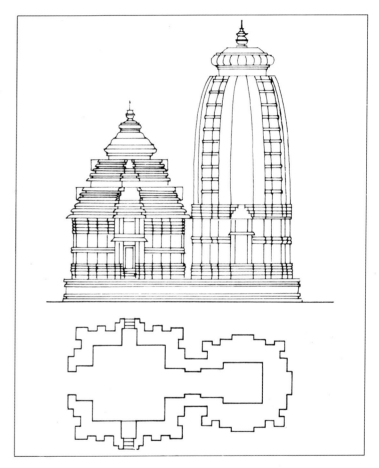

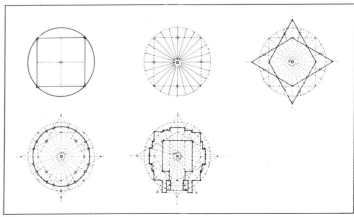

116. Bhuvanesvar, temple of
Parasuramesvara, detail of the
sikhara.

117. Bhuvanesvar, temple of
Parasuramesvara.

120. *Bhuvanesvar, temple of
Brahmesvara, plan, elevation, and
section (from Volwahsen, 1969).*

121. *Bhuvanesvar, temple of
Brahmesvara, axonometric drawing
(from Volwahsen, 1969).*

122. *Bhuvanesvar, temple of
Lingaraja, schematic elevations of the
two principal buildings (from Debala
Mitra, 1961).*

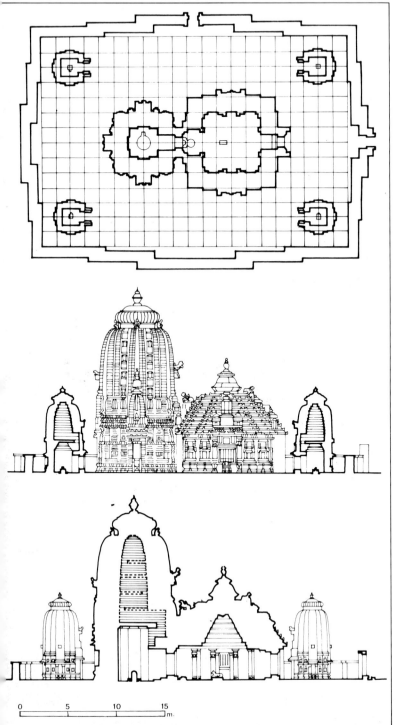

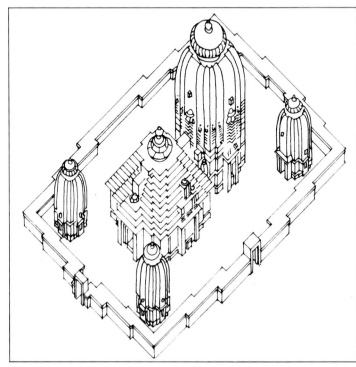

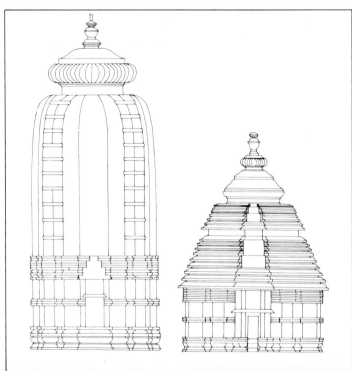

124. Modhera, temple of Surya.
125. Modhera, temple of Surya; in
the foreground, the brick terrace.

126. Modhera, temple of Surya; in
the foreground, the brick terrace.

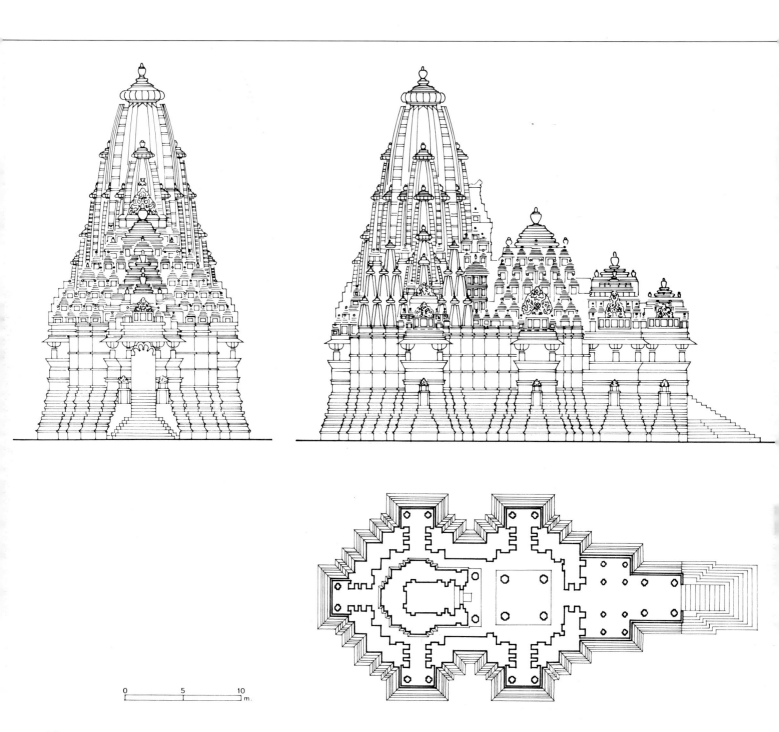

127. Khajuraho, temple of Kandariya Mahadeo, elevations and plan (from Volwahsen, 1969).

0   5   10
m.

tion to a foreign cult of fire, will persist in time. Different but important elements of this can be found in Kashmir temples, which at times—according to certain scholars—take on aspects related to Western art of the Gothic period. These are obviously superficial and ill-founded impressions, but they serve to underscore the effect that geometric motifs may suggest when placed side by side with those of Classical derivation. In any case, the architectural development of Kashmir is a chapter in itself in the history of Indian art. One need only recall the renowned and enigmatic temple of Harvan, with its characteristic terra-cotta wall coverings and its exploitation of an irregular space for the platform; and also the famous Temple of the Sun at Martand, dating to the eighth century.

Great temple architecture begins, in any case, around the middle of the Gupta period, and its surviving examples are especially numerous in the western regions. All Gupta temples are relatively small and have flat roofs. Construction is in brick but without the use of lime, which indicates a particular stage in technique subject to further development. It is significant that one of the best examples, the sixth-century temple at Deogarh near Jhansi, employs iron pegs to hold the masonry together, an expedient that permitted the erection of a small tower over the sacred chapel. The heart of the temple—as is always true of any Indian temple—was formed by a small cell; closed except for the entrance, it was called the *garbha griha*, since it was here that the principal and holiest image was kept. By means of a vestibule called the *antarba*, the cell communicated with the *mandapa*, where the faithful carried out their devotions. Originally, the *mandapa* was a separate building. This room was in its turn preceded, as one entered from the outside, by an *ardhamandapa* portico. This succession and linking of different rooms, prescribed by the texts, is preserved throughout the centuries, along with the custom of leaving the main cell free of decoration; only the proportions and minor details vary. If we keep in mind, however, the extent of Indian territory, the variety of cultures it contains, and the very long period of architectural activity, we must concede that there is a certain uniformity in temple architecture.

One of the oldest temples for the phase we are considering is undoubtedly the one known as No. 17 at Sanchi. It has been definitely dated to the fifth century A.D. and is square in plan, with a columned portico that recalls a Greek temple, though this does not imply an actual derivation from or dependence on Greek models. Temple No. 18, which follows it in numerical sequence, has been largely destroyed; all that remains of it are tall columns surmounted by a lintel, giving a curious combined effect of classicism and modernity. It may have been topped by a low curvilinear tower, but there is little basis for this hypothesis, which anyway does not resolve the problem of variations and types of temple structures presented by many incomplete temples. It is certain that the simplest solution, the flat roof, did not satisfy Indian taste, even though others offered serious technical difficulties. The preference, for symbolic reasons, was a projecting roof with jutting rows

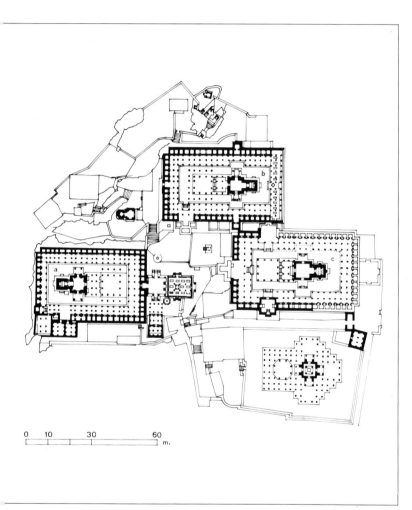

135. *Rajputana, Mount Abu,
complex of Jain sanctuaries: a) plan
of the temple of Vimala; b) plan of
the temple of Tejapal; c) plan of the
temple of Adinatha (from Volwahsen,
1969).*

136. *Rajputana, Mount Abu, temple
of Dilwara, interior of the* mandapa.

137. *Rajputana, Mount Abu, temple of Dilwara, interior of the dome.*

138. *Puri, temple of Jagannatha.*

139. *Gangaikondacholapuram, temple of Brihadisvara.*

140. *Belur, temple of Cennakesava.*

of stones placed on successive levels, on which smaller buildings seem to rise, their presence modulating the space into continuous denticulations. The surface tension is broken and the building acquires mass and body in an exceptional and pleasing way.

The development of the Indian temple from the sixth to the eighth century can be easily reconstructed—though not without uncertainties— from the important architectural complex constituted by the cities of Badami, Aihole, and Pattadakal, the political and religious capitals of the Chalukya rulers. In Aihole, the temple of Durga, the great goddess of war, is probably the earliest known example of the sikhara temple with a curvilinear roof, of which we will speak later, along with that of Laksmana at Sirpur. Unfortunately, the latter is completely in ruins and difficult to reconstruct in its original form. The other sikharas at Aihole are dated slightly later, and the problem of the development of Indian temples begins to be complicated by chronological uncertainties.

We are unable to properly place works in other regions of India, with the exception of those in the Tamil area ruled by the Pallavas, political rivals of the Rashtrakutas and at the same time their emulators in the field of architectural construction.

There is, however, no need here to concern ourselves with political conflicts between little-known dynasties in medieval India, even though such conflicts were important and profound. Yet it is an interesting fact that Vikramaditya II, who won Kanchipuram from the Pallavas and made large donations to the Brahmins, the poor, and the temples of the city, carried away with him to Kanara a number of great Tamil artists and architects, to whom he gave special honors. Among these men we find mention of Chattara, Revadi, and Ovajja; we know too that Gunda, who was responsible for the construction of the temple of Virupaksha, was originally from the south. Such information shows a tendency to mitigate the anonymity of artists and testifies to the fame that some of them enjoyed. It may also help to explain the spread of technical and stylistic solutions from one region to another, over great distances, and the reception accorded to the style (or at least the taste) of the Pallavas, even outside their own territory and independent of political vicissitudes.

Indian architectural treatises distinguish two principal types of temples: the *nāgara* and the *dravida.* Both words have an ethnic reference, but in essence they mean the northern and southern style, respectively. Such a classification is not entirely justified: French scholars have shown that temples of the *nāgara* type and sikharas (a word meaning peak, point, or flame) are found not only in Madras but originated in the Deccan region, where we find them at Aihole and Pattadakal. They are present too in Orissa, Kathiawar, and Rajputana—that is to say, in central areas or ones marginal to that implied by the term *nāgara*. Many writers have chosen to keep the stylistic definition found in the Indian texts, eliminating only the *vesara* category that refers to the extreme south. It is preferable, however, to

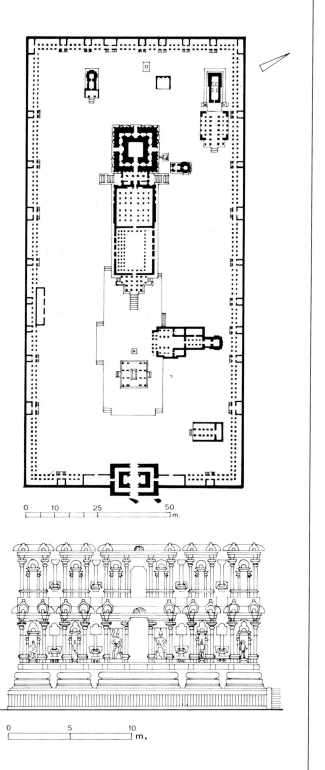

141. Tanjore, temple of Brihadisvara, entrance portal.

142. Tanjore, temple of Brihadisvara, ground plan and section of the cell (from Volwahsen, 1969).

143. Halebid, temple of Hoysalesvara.

144. Halebid, temple of Hoysalesvara, detail of the exterior.

145. Somnathpur, temple of Kesava.
146. Somnathpur, temple of Kesava, section and plan (from Volwahsen, 1969).

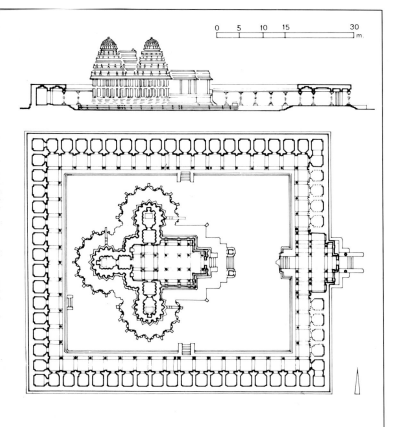

replace these subdivisions with a morphological classification relating primarily to temple roofs, separated as follows: temples with curvilinear roofs (sikharas); temples with pyramidal (or prismatic) roofs; temples with cylindrical (or barrel-vaulted) roofs.

Unfortunately, the destruction wreaked by the Muslims drastically reduced the amount of architectural evidence available in the north. Though this irreparable loss makes it difficult indeed to trace northern developments in style, it is possible to examine these three types of temples.

a) Sikharas

It is possible that curvilinear towered roofs may be related to very ancient bamboo constructions—reed coverings that served to protect Vedic altars.[8] This hypothesis, though plausible, has no true scientific or critical basis. On the other hand, it is certain that the construction of the curvilinear roof—with its superimposed horizontal moldings and its vertical ones, whether rounded in the amalaka fashion or angular, effects which soften the harshness of the transition from the rectangular base to the roundness at the top—is connected with the use of baked bricks. In some cases, a crude brick structure was incised in order to make it more elaborate and definitive, confirming the Indian custom of cutting as a means of achieving architectural form. The roof, rising above the often cubical structure of the base, appears to result from the superimposition of horizontal molded cornices intersected by vertical bands of protuberances and sockets, rounded or with sharp edges. In plan, these moldings show a polylobate motif, approximately cruciform, that perhaps derives—with many modifications—from Persepolitan capitals.[9] The taste governing the sikhara is obviously for a very compact architectural mass, isolated and capable of producing a strong tension on the surrounding aerial space. It is more a plastic taste than an architectural one, and expresses its fancy in a minute elaboration of the enormous ogival dome that rises toward the sky.

The development of the sikhara can be logically summarized as follows. The progressive elevation and narrowing of the ogival dome (generically called the *chapra*) is combined with an interest in the form itself. This means that the elongation and reduction of the roof are the effect of an upward surge that can easily be related to an increased mystical component and a resulting perfection in technique. This explanation may be obvious and partial, but it is certain that the multiplication of vertical grooves derives from a clear wish to accentuate the upward direction of the roof. On the other hand, the appreciation of the ogival form as a plastic motif is undeniable; this wish to emphasize the upward effect of the whole is intensified by the addition of smaller sikharas of varying height, joined to and surrounding the central tower and seeming to animate, on various levels, the thrust toward the sky. Once again, we find a demonstration of that characteristic Indian taste, which in the sphere of the figurative arts stops short of true abstraction only through a series of connections that prevent

147. *Somnathpur, temple of Kesava.*

148. Somnathpur, temple of Kesava, detail.

149. Somnathpur, temple of Kesava, detail of sculptured decoration on the outer wall of the cell.

150. Konarak, temple of Surya, view of the jagamohan.

it from fully exploiting the theoretical presuppositions at its disposal. It is this same taste that determines an appreciation for the ogival form and multiplies it at different levels as it rises toward the sky.

It is curious but not inexplicable that the most beautiful temples of this type, with multiple ogives, number among others those at Khajuraho: the temples of Kandariya Mahadeo, Visvanatha, and Laksmana, for example, are enriched by a monumental series of sculptures renowned for their innumerable erotic motifs. Their explicitness is not likely to be enjoyed by those who are unprepared for it or are not sufficiently uninhibited. In reality, the ascending movement of these temples, connected with the orgiastic rites practiced by the Chandella rulers, expresses a precise and basically acceptable moral lesson: life offers countless pleasures, among them the predominant ones of sex and love, but it is not infinite; it can be prolonged by magical practices and suitable orgiastic rites, but it is also appropriate, once a certain limit has been reached, to prepare oneself for the last, definitive journey, one that will truly be without return and carry the person to his dispersal in the Absolute. Even the Temple of the Sun at Konarak—which, had it been completed, would have reached a height of over 390 feet—was decorated with erotic scenes. The *mandapa* (originally a hypostyle portico that led into the actual temple lying behind it, and later to become a building in itself, though always subordinate to the temple) attained a height of 230 feet at Konarak. It is conceived as an enormous solar chariot, whose wheels, finely executed and carved, display the figures of amorous couples (*mithunas*) in their hubs. This grandiose solution is in imitation of the *raths* (small temples in the form of processional chariots) erected in various periods and in various forms. Often monolithic, they may also have represented royal chariots, as at Mamallapuram, where the huge boulders with which the site was strewn furnished material that could be artistically transformed into isolated figures and small temples, the principal one being the Dharmaraja *rath*—the royal chariot.

The lesser towers that form a crown for the main one are called *anga-sikharas*, and can be arranged like isolated structures—almost as foreparts—in relation to the projections of the various faces of the main tower, as we find in the Jain temples of Satrunjaya, dating from the sixteenth century; or else as multiplications of the tower motif and joined to the principal one (a motif known as multiple towers). With this description, we have virtually exhausted this analysis of the sikhara construction, and it only remains to note that the multiple-tower system emerged in the ninth century and immediately proved itself more flexible than the other. Better suited to a wide range of effects, it finally assumes greater aesthetic validity, since it produces a blossoming of curved lines that almost flow from the central amalaka. The motif itself is especially widespread in western regions of India, and according to some scholars can be traced in plan to a complex system of circles inscribed in squares and intersecting among themselves—thus to a geometric basis.

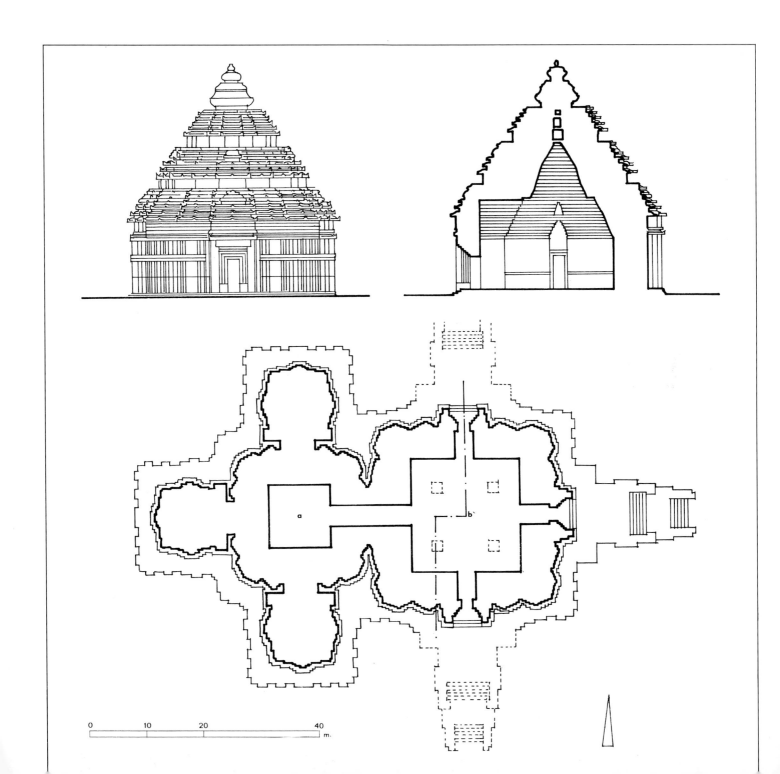

151. Konarak, temple of Surya, elevation and section of the jagamohan; *plan of the* garbha griha *(a) and of the* jagamohan *(b) (from Volwahsen, 1969).*

a

b

0   10   20   40
                                      m.

IX. Khajuraho, temple of Kandariya.

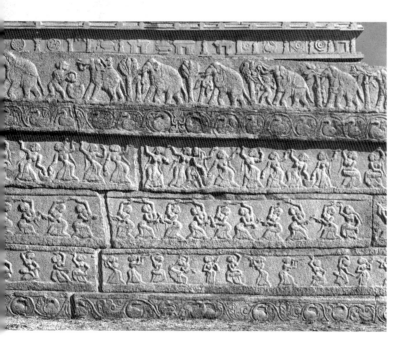

158. *Vijayanagar (Hampi), temple of Vitthalasvami, view of a* mandapa.
159. *Vijayanagar (Hampi), temple of the Mahanavami Dibba, council hall.*

160. *Vijayanagar (Hampi), Mahanavami Dibba, detail of sculptured friezes on the terrace of the building.*

b) Vimānas

Temples with high pyramidal or prismatic roofs are generally called *vimānas*. According to French scholars, there are precedents for the southern *vimāna* in the pictorial images of Ajanta's Cave No. 1, which dates back to the sixth century A.D., and in the sculptured ones in the *Descent of the Ganges* at Mamallapuram. The first surviving example, however, would be the Dharmaraja *rath*, also at Mamallapuram, which we have already mentioned. The type becomes established about the middle of the eighth century, both with the Kailasanath at Ellora and—for constructed architecture—with that at Kanchipuram. Though it can vary considerably, it is essentially formed by a central structure, square in plan, over which rises the pyramidal roof of steps forming the planes on which what we might call "miniaturized" reproductions of buildings are placed in a rigorously regular fashion. These reproductions slowly diminish in size as they proceed toward the crown (square or polygonal) of the truncated pyramid. On these same buildings in miniature, which assume the form of ordinary pavilions, the *kūdu* (false horseshoe-shaped window) is often represented. This motif, obviously arranged in parallel horizontal rows with regard to the placing of the pavilions, becomes a characteristic decorative element that succeeds in animating the surface. It should be immediately pointed out that an analysis of the lesser ornamental motifs, featuring animals and plants, confirms the significance of these constructions as cosmic mountains sustaining human habitations.

A comparison between the Dharmaraja *rath* at Mamallapuram (36 feet in height) and the *vimāna* at Tanjore, one of the finest examples and much larger in size, shows the enormous development of this type of temple. At Tanjore, there are thirteen levels instead of three and the pyramidal shape is clearer. The use of the *kūdu* as an ornamental element is infinitely more pronounced, even though far removed, for aesthetic reasons, from the prescriptions imposed by the texts. The Tanjore *vimāna*, known as the Rajrajesvara temple, is a very daring construction: it reached a height of 180 feet and was topped by a single immense stone whose weight has been calculated at 80 tons. The *vimāna* type tends, however, to become heavy and clumsy as a result of the efforts of artists and patrons to increase the proportions of the building excessively. This leads therefore to a progressive aridity in this type, though we must remember that its use was spread over almost the whole of Indian territory. Particularly curious are the mixed types, combining elements of the sikhara with others of the *vimāna*. Primarily to be found in the Mysore region, they are always crowned by an amalaka.

c) Gopuras

Temples with pyramidal roofs, or *gopuras*, form part of the temple enclosure. Originally, they were very simple in form and connected with the gates of ancient cities, but during the medieval phase they became monumental constructions that attained extraordinary height and, in their amassing of

162. Vijayanagar (Hampi),
"underground" temple.

materials, took on an isolated grandeur. Their form is distinctly prismatic, with superimposed planes, and slightly tapering toward the top. They constitute a characteristic element in the landscape of southern India and are among the most original constructions of those areas.

In addition, the inventive capacity of southern architects is confirmed by the star-shaped plans of the temples at Halebid, and Belur, commissioned by the Hoysala rulers, in which the sculptural decoration, confined to particular areas, exhibits highly studied effects of light and shadow, calculated for the intense luminosity of the south and even for the leaden light of the monsoon season.

As for the development of the *gopura*, there is not much to say except to point out that it established itself primarily during the thirteenth and fourteenth centuries, and that its extended height sometimes produced an excessively attenuated effect, approaching the simplest form of the tower surmounted by a canopy.

Summary of Indian Architecture

Thanks to the Jains, Indian architecture later discovered the whiteness of marble and the open-work effects that could be achieved with it, but went on to exhaust itself in the more or less successful repetition of created types. The violent crisis produced by the clash with Islam, the historical vicissitudes of this immense world unable to independently express a true capacity for unification (despite the experience of the Mogul Empire), and the increasing contact with Western colonial powers, spread a kind of benumbed torpor over the whole subcontinent. New and daring philosophical and mystical experiments were not enough to rouse a population ill-prepared to recognize the origins and reasons for an oppressive authority (whether local or foreign), and which it did not even think of opposing. Architecture passed into the hands of the Muslim faithful, and the local religious impetus was lost in a thousand streams of individual and group action without succeeding in renewing itself.

Thus, we may consider the great architecture of Hindu India as exhausted by the end of the sixteenth century. Here and there we may still find ingenious insights, advanced solutions, and characteristic geometric patterns. But such examples have no echo beyond themselves. They remain isolated, and are often rediscovered accidentally, or almost so, by scholars or experts in search of secondary monuments or of details that are usually overlooked, or by those who set out to express a different point of view. In the midst of the repetitive monotony, there thus emerged suggestions and incomplete or scarcely realized attempts that nevertheless were not enough to generate a revival: Indian architecture had exhausted itself. In the long period of its prosperity, however, it had accumulated an enormous sum of experience, which—and here we touch on a paradox—is poorly known; the architecture and in general all the artistic activity of India is considered to be "other" than the taste and aesthetic aspirations of the

163. *Vijayanagar (Hampi), Lotus Mahal.*

164. *Chidambaram, temple of Siva Natesvara.*

165. *Vellore, fortress temple.*

167. Srirangam, temple of Vishnu, detail of the garuda-mandapa.

168. Madura, temple of Siva and Minaksi, plan of the whole and section of the southern gopura *(from Volwahsen, 1969).*

modern world. Its enormous religious content constitutes a sufficient handicap for the majority of contemporary critics and art lovers, while by contrast it is precisely in its complicated symbolism and underlying mysticism that many of those persons well disposed toward it seek the *raison d'être* of Indian architecture. Nevertheless, even granting the relative technical poverty of an art that succeeds in arousing respect despite all preconceptions, we will try to summarize its aesthetic side, expressed in intense and prolonged creative activity, by considering some of its key points.

The architect, the patron, and the public itself for whom the work of art was created virtually constituted an inseparable unity forming part of a solid chain of tradition that went back ultimately to divine inspiration. It was no accident that one of those who had worked on the Kailasanath temple at Ellora, contemplating the miracle of the work just completed, asked himself in wonder: "How was I able to do so much?"[10]

Actually, for the Indian creative intellect, there did not exist any opposition between subject and object. The work, the artist, and those who enjoyed the created forms constituted a unity that, by means of the visible part, succeeded also in merging with those invisible vibrations (*adrsta*) that had accompanied the creative process. The love for architectural form in itself—always logical and geometric—dominated all the sculptural creations that adorned it and which, deprived of this support, would have lost their full value. On the other hand, the proportions of the architectural structure, rigidly fixed in precise, systematic relationships, constituted the "breath" (*prana*) of the work itself, which lives—indeed is truly a work of art—only if the rhythm and throb of its lines succeed in being united with the vital movement of its creators. The theoretical units of Indian architecture can practically be traced back to the altar (even the stupa is an altar, in the metaphorical sense), the pillar (and many temples have the meaning and magical function of the pillar), the mountain, cavern (or cave), and finally the door. All are symbolic elements, but in each of them the artist must achieve a point of attraction and concentration in relation to the movement of the pilgrim or officiant obliged to follow a prescribed route. The ideal axis of the stupa, for example, would be the invisible pivot for circumambulation. For this reason, on the strip of the drum supporting the dome, the Greco-Buddhist images of the north take on a perspective that we call rotating, since they tend to remain valid from all vantage points granted to persons performing *pradakshinā* (ritual circumambulation). The relation between vision in motion and architectural and plastic structure is thus a strong one. We find it again even in Hindu temples, where the images are placed in such a way as to offer themselves time and again to the eye of the worshiper.

"In this concentric, concentrating perambulation the devotee sees the piers and recesses of the walls together with their sculptures. He feels their impact, as the buttresses project and display the images. These buttresses are called *ratha*, meaning chariot. It is as though they were being driven

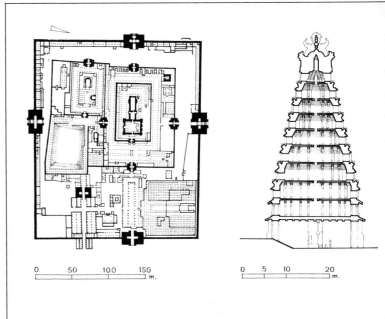

out from the center of the monument, each buttress in its respective direction, pulling its own bulk and the images stationed thereon."[11] The structural masses project and carry with them the images found on them. The Hindu temple was created in relation both to a movement toward the center (that of men), and to a monumental space that seems to obey a centrifugal movement with the capacity to explode from the center and dispose the parts of the temple and secondary buildings in such a way as to offer an isolated yet simultaneously total vision. Thus it moves and "breathes" according to the movement of the individual pilgrim and his way of looking, breathing, and thinking. It is, as a well-known French scholar has remarked, a "cinema of stone." And, the fact that the texts sometimes place the construction of ritual chariots side by side with the more complex construction of temples (and vice versa) shows that the aesthetic basis of Hindu sacred architecture is movement. Thus, each Indian architectural creation, based on geometry and light, on the movement of masses and the real but slow movement of men, expresses in reality a form that emanates from within, that composes and disposes, to create a *vyaktavyakta* (a form that must exist); in the sphere of culture that created it, this form is the most logical and obvious synthesis of the many highly varied requirements that prompted its birth.

In medieval Hindu architecture, the Indian creative genius reached the summit of its own power and logical rigor. It is now up to us to find a universal aesthetic measure that will allow us to evaluate it more effectively.

Ceylon

The island of Sri Lanka, formerly known as Ceylon (Selān in the local language, but Lankā or Tāmraparnī, in classical Indian designations), lies at the extreme southern end of the Indian subcontinent. As such, it should be classified as part of the Indian world from which it derives, above all for its religious thought. However, in the field of the figurative arts in general and in architecture in particular, the island has had considerable importance and an extraordinary autonomy. It is for these reasons that Ceylon can be considered and studied as an artistic area in itself, even though clearly complementary to India. To begin with, Ceylon still remains a Buddhist stronghold, thus ensuring a linear and prolonged development of the architecture inspired by this religion. Of the island's inhabitants, only the Tamils, who were recently estimated to represent 30 per cent of the local population, were adherents of Hinduism, taking their inspiration— albeit in an independent manner—from forms prevailing in southern India. The peripheral and relatively protected geographic position of Ceylon shielded the island from events that convulsed the neighboring subcontinent, while accentuating to some extent the conservatism characteristic of islands. But these factors are only partly responsible for the independence and originality of Singhalese art. A particular sensitivity to spatial values, and the presence of an unmistakable taste made up of different components,

174. Anhilvara-Patan, Han Sarovar,
detail of the decoration for a well.

XIII. Vishnupur, temple of Madan
Mohan.

175. Jodhpur (Mandor), Rajput funerary monument.

178. *Trichur (Kerala), round temple.*
179. *Trichur (Kerala), temple of Siva.*

are more notable reasons for Singhalese artistic autonomy and for the influence that Ceylon's architectural forms exerted on centers in Magna India.

The origins of Singhalese architecture, according to tradition, must be traced to the introduction of Buddhism on the island, which local chronicles tell us occurred with the visit of Asoka's son, Mahinda, about the middle of the third century B.C. The ecclesiastical basis of Buddhism (the *samgha*)—that is, the associative essence of a religion that did not originally have transcendental or protective elements suitable for transforming the doctrine into a system and rule of life to mollify the individual in the face of the anguish of existence—required, among other things, monastic constructions and focal points for the cult. This obviously was translated into an urge to build, to meet the indispensable construction needs connected not only with the very nature of religious life, but also with organizational needs and with the fact that Buddhism alone formulated its possibilities for success on the cohabitation of monks and on continual proselytizing. The activity of Devanam-Piyatissa—the Singhalese ruler contemporary with Asoka and a convert of the missionaries sent by the Maurya emperor—was precisely directed to the building of stupas and monasteries. The Thuparama *dagaba* (stupa) at Anuradhapura would seem to go back, in its original form, to this period. Tradition adds, however, that the Mahiyangana *dagaba* in the province of Uva, and the Girikandi (now Tiriyay) *dagaba* on the northeast coast of the island, also belong to the same time.

In reality, the source of inspiration for the oldest monuments in Ceylon should be sought in the evidence offered by the primitive schools of central India (Bharhut, Sanchi, even Buddh Gaya). Of all such monuments, the most characteristic is the stupa. But Ceylon combines the work commemorating the Buddha (the architectural projection of the whole universe as seen "from outside"; that is, from a dimension, we might say, alien to human sensory experience) with a type of structure that hinges on the cult of the tree of Buddha's Enlightenment—a different approach with a symbolic significance similar to that of the stupa. The building in question is called the *bodhighara*, and though rare, constitutes an interesting alternative possibility for symbolic construction on a Buddhist basis. The *bodhighara*, not unknown in India, must have had a greater importance in Ceylon than in the continental area.

As for the stupa, the persistence of that old Indian form—with its hemispherical dome known as the *anda*—is not due to backwardness. It is, as we have said, the fruit of a spatial sensibility that prefers the tension of the geometrically perfect curved line to the more symbolically charged modifications that evolved successively on the Indian mainland. In addition to its skyline, the plastic volume of the hemisphere attracted and satisfied the taste of Singhalese architects; hence the influence that the stupa of Ceylon exercised on the bell-shaped, hemispherically topped forms of Magna India from Java to Thailand. Naturally, there are exceptions (for example, a

181. *Anuradhapura, remains of the Brazen palace.*
182. *Anuradhapura, Mahathupa (Ruvanvali).*

183. *Nalanda, Gedige, Tantric Buddhist chapel.*
184. *Polonnaruwa, Thuparama.*
185. *Polonnaruwa, sanctuary of Siva in the Chola style.*

twelfth-century stupa in the form of a graduated pyramid of seven levels), but by and large this influence holds true. On the other hand, that the choice of the hemispherical form was determined by visual taste is proved both by the solutions adopted for the votive rings (the celebrated umbrellas)—which only become heavy when translated into brick, being transformed into a kind of molded conical spiral—and by the projections or foreparts (*vāhalkadas*) of the enormous stupas of Anuradhapura. Flanked by stelae that are surmounted by animal forms facing outward, they determine the approach to the building for arriving worshipers. These projections are placed at the four cardinal points, in accordance with the pattern of orientation customary for this type of monument. The oldest of these monuments, so far as we know from reliable historical evidence, is the Abhayagiri, north of Anuradhapura. Originally, it was not of great size. It was, however, enlarged by King Gajabahu I in the second century A.D., attaining a diameter of 354 feet and a height that must have approached 347 feet (now, with its cusp broken, it is only 243 feet high). Its *vāhalkadas* are also from the second century A.D., which shows that this distinctive characteristic of the Singhalese stupa was already fully formed in ancient times—a notable divergence from continental patterns.

Lesser stupas were contained within circular sanctuaries called *cetiyāgāras*, covered by a wooden cupola that rested on a perimeter of columns planted a short distance from the edge of the stupa. Two or three wider concentric rings of columns placed around the one upholding the cupola served to support a roof that also rested on a continuous wall placed between the two outer colonnades. An interest in spherical volume and curved lines (or rather in circles and semicircles) is obvious. In more developed examples, the outer wall may be decorated with ornamental motifs that chiefly take advantage of the continuous surface; or it can—as at Madirigiri in the eighth century—be in line with the outer colonnade and assume the form of a stone balustrade (derived from the classical ones at Sanchi). For this type of construction as well, which in Ceylon continues until the fifteenth century, the local development differs from that on the continent.

The cult of the tree of Buddha's Enlightenment led to a strange symbiosis between a living, natural element, conditioned by the needs of its own existence—the tree—and the need for isolation, for making the sacred concrete, for the spatial definition required by the cult. The *Mahāvamsa*, one of the most famous Singhalese Buddhist texts, tells us that the Bodhi Tree (of Enlightenment) in the Mahavihara at Anuradhapura was planted on a raised terrace, surrounded by a *vedikā* (balustrade) with a single *torana* (open gate) on the north side; four pillars, each supporting a wheel, the chief symbol of Buddha's Law (*dharmacakra*), were placed at the *torana* and the three secondary open entrances at the other cardinal points. From this type—which imitates the celebrated one at Buddh Gaya—derives a hypostyle pavilion with two entrances (north and south), and having a low ornamental roof and rectangular plan, at whose center rose the platform

186. *Polonnaruwa, Lankatilaka,*
house-temple for the image of Buddha;
to the right, the Kiri Vehera dagaba.

designed to hold the sacred tree, obviously placed under the open sky.

We cannot verify the truth of assertions in the *Mahāvamsa* concerning the many radical changes that took place with the passage of centuries. We can, however, note the perfect preservation—for this type of construction— of the recently discovered Nillakgama *bodhighara* (in Kurunagala), dating to the eighth or ninth century. The use of "moon stones"—that is, of symbolic semicircles of stones placed before the entrances—is not limited to *bodhigharas*, but constantly recurs as a truly Singhalese characteristic before the outer approaches (passages with symbolic significance) of sacred buildings. We do not know how many *bodhigharas* there were in Ceylon, nor if the alternative that this building offered to the stupa was only a potential one that was seldom exploited. A comparison of the description in the *Mahāvamsa* with the surviving example implies that a slow transformation has clearly detached the original type of the *bodhighara*—very close to the stupa, even though the tree is substituted for the reliquary construction that forms the true stupa—from that of the stupa itself. The result is that the *bodhighara* takes on an appearance in which the vital needs of the tree—axis of the world, symbol of the Law, and reminiscence of Buddha— prevail over the symbolic values.

The architectural development of the island tends, for several reasons, gradually to abandon the use of wood, whether for royal residences, for monastic buildings, or finally for the superstructures of various buildings whose foundations and access ramps were of stone. Brick constructions, the oldest of which goes back to the eighth century, acquire the name of *gedigēs* (a term, according to the *Rūpas-siddhi-sanne*, equivalent to the Pali form *giñjakāvasatha*, reserved, as Buddhaghosa states, for constructions entirely of brick), a name soon extended to stone constructions with vaulted roofs. The chapels or house-temples for images of Buddha—called *gandals* from the name of the chamber reserved for Buddha in the garden of Jetavana, or more often referred to as *pilimages*—reveal by their growing numbers over the years an ever greater interest on the part of the faithful in the cult of icons (if we may call it so). It is likely that the architects of Ceylon, in planning the first *gandals*, intended to reproduce the pavilion-room of Jetavana. If this is true, it indicates a deliberate local desire to appropriate, so to speak, the holy places of Buddhist tradition. Such an action is typical of outlying areas animated by intense faith. In any case, the *gandal* was originally a square or rectangular building, with a single room preceded by a forepart. Naturally, the type became more complicated with the passage of time, also because of the upsurge in popularity of the cult of images. A *mandapa* was added in the form of an antistructure that acted as a portico but was also a temple in itself.

In practice, the *gandal*, having become the classical Buddhist *patimagārā* and a true sanctuary, ended by resuming, at least in its essential lines, the characteristic structure of Hindu temples in India, consisting of three parts: the inner sanctum or true chapel (*garbha griha*); the structure that precedes

it; and the *mandapa*, a temple structure serving also as a portico.

Naturally, the appearance and size of these structures vary considerably, and—as at Anuradhapura—there is no lack of arrangements of the "quincuncial" kind, in which the major edifice is placed at the center. We thus return to patterns of arrangement that belong to the Indian world. It should be noted that in the late period a particular characteristic of these Singhalese constructions is that they are built entirely of brick. Only the molded stylobates—sometimes also in brick—are, with a certain frequency, of stone, as are the door jambs, which are likewise molded.

In addition, the architecture of Ceylon includes individual and collective dwellings. Vast monastic complexes surround Anuradhapura, to the west of which we find monastic cells (now erroneously called palaces) that were most likely used for meditation. Apart from the remains of the Brazen palace, the amusement garden, and the dam for the artificial Tisavava Lake (built in the third century A.D.), the city included numerous stone baths and its famous sacred buildings. The urban layout, perhaps an involuntary one, thus established a central area for habitation and for political and commercial activity that was virtually encircled by monastic establishments. It has been pointed out, however, that there is a clear difference between official and individual dwellings and community ones. According to the tradition, some of the first monastic dwellings were as severely austere as simple caves, while others were magnificently rich. Such was the case of the residence donated to Mahinda by General Dighasanda, a building that according to the *Mahavamsa* towered against the sky and was "enclosed by beautiful walls and adorned with superb staircases."

Very probably the so-called Elephant Stables are the remains of a splendid building of this kind, built at Anuradhapura by Kanit-Thatissa, and later rebuilt by Mahinda II (A.D. 777-797) at a cost of 300,000 pieces of gold. The edifice, which included pillars and stylobates of exceptional size, was doubtless capable of vying with the most sumptuous royal dwellings. The habit of donating sumptuous houses continued for a long time, without excluding the presence of hermitages and cave dwellings (later to be adorned by the piety of the faithful) for anyone who sought sanctity in the form of a total rejection of society and the world. Notable examples are the Kaludiyapokuna cave near Mihintale, the Arankale cave, and the group of large caves at Dambulla, all later provided with brick walls or transformed into shrines. As for monasteries, it should be mentioned that the principal part of each complex was the *uposathagara*, the large meeting hall where the monks gathered on auspicious days for the ceremony of public confession and to discuss the proceedings of their order. Important ceremonies and festivals were celebrated in the *uposathagara*, whose best surviving example is at Polonnaruwa and is also described in the *Mahavamsa*; its façade was characterized by lanceolate windows. Here the central hall is surrounded by corridors and service rooms (chapels and spaces designed to hold sacred objects and implements). It is polystyle, and at its center has a two-level

raised structure for the oldest monk, responsible for the discipline and spiritual order of the entire monastery. A curious fact to be noted is that the monasteries of Ceylon were equipped from the beginning with hygienic facilities greatly superior to those in India; the sewers and water pipes for the large baths constantly appear next to monasteries. The baths, called *pokunas* in Singhalese (from the Sanskrit *puskarani*), are rectangular in plan (though occasionally circular), and were sometimes dug out of the rock. Granite was later used to cover the floors and walls. The best example is the pair of baths (a double swimming pool) situated in the Abhayagiri area, at Vosihara near Anuradhapura, and popularly called Kuttam Pokuna (which means double or twin bath). The two tanks, contained in a single enclosure with six stairways for access, are equal in width, but differ in length and depth (length, 143 feet and 98 1/2 feet respectively; depth at center, 19 1/2 feet for the larger, 15 feet for the smaller). Both are bordered by a stone parapet projecting over the encased strip of flooring that acts as a frame and edge (or beach) for the two pools. Highly planned in all its details and with hydraulic installations that show great ingenuity, the Kuttam Pokuna is one of the most important architectural works on the island. The Archaeological Department has made significant restorations of the complex, returning it to its original elegant simplicity.

The presence of large hospitals, side by side with the major monasteries, completes the picture of Singhalese architecture. Their existence reflects the diligent civil and social life of the population, which is strongly united by a desire for autonomy and by an effective solidarity that seems to replace the essentially compassionate Buddhist *karuna* by a feeling much closer to active Christian *caritas*.

It is highly probable that Ceylon's geographic position, its formulation of doctrine, and its technical interest in architectural works, were accompanied—in determining the island's wide influence on architectural trends in Southeast Asia—by this activism of its people. It is something easily appreciated by coreligionists who, being more concerned with the contingencies of human life than are the orthodox extremists, likewise wished to react against the inert renunciation suggested by the law of karma.

Mario Bussagli

143

Introduction

The great span of Southeast Asia and the countries it contains are often referred to as Magna India or Farther India, appellations that serve to underscore the significant influence of India upon the cultures of this vast zone. Contacts with the Indian world directly affected Indonesia and all of Indochina except for the territory of Tonkin and the northern parts of Laos and Vietnam. The gradual result was the transition of the affected regions from levels of culture that were scarcely developed to the plane of complete civilization. As Mario Bussagli has stated elsewhere: "The progressive expansion of Indian civilization, its absorption on the part of populations very different among themselves, and the successive transformation of this foreign influence in the process of its adaptation to various local needs often produced unexpected phenomena, particularly in the field of the figurative arts."[1]

The sporadic penetration of this Indian expansion was peaceful in character, but from the cultural standpoint its impact led to the highly important phenomena Bussagli describes. Archaeological evidence indicates that as early as the first century A.D. the Indians were pushing forward by sea into the areas under discussion, following the coasts and venturing as far as the Sonda Islands. Some scholars believe that this movement was precipitated by pressures exerted by an expanding population or by the missionary vocation of Buddhism; more simply, they can be attributed to the requirements of commerce. The Roman world, especially in the imperial era, exerted a continual demand on the Indian East for pearls, perfumes, silk, precious stones, myrrh, and incense. Consequently, an active trade was established between the Romanized Middle East and India; the Indians searched for gold and spices along the coasts of Southeast Asia, which their special knowledge of monsoons permitted them to reach easily, and here they founded commercial settlements that in time grew into trade centers. A colonization of an economic kind emerged that was supported neither by political aims nor military force; it did not therefore take on the nature of a conquest nor seek to establish hegemony or economic monopoly. Mixed marriages between Indian men and local women likewise contributed to closer and more stable ties between the two populations.

With the introduction of the alphabet and the Sanskrit language, Indian thought became widespread. At the same time there was a propagation of two other elements of Indian life—the organizational model of the state, hinging on the monarchy, and Indian religious beliefs. In the field of art, the ensuing dependence on India is so obvious as to seem a common denominator, albeit within the autonomy and individuality of local styles.

As we have said, the only regions of Indochina to remain outside the Indian sphere were the territory of Tonkin and the northern parts of Laos and Vietnam. These areas experienced, in particular ways, the political and cultural domination of China. Unlike the Indian influence, the Chinese expansion was a true military conquest, obviously hated by the populations who suffered under its yoke. Despite a number of revolts, which generally took place at times of crisis for the imperial government, Tonkin remained a Chinese province until A.D. 938. In Vietnam the Chinese influence was so complete that its imprint remained a predominant factor until the beginning of the twentieth century.

We can summarize the permanent characteristics of the historical equilibrium in the area we are now considering in the following manner: (1) The Indianized states were independent of the political structures existing in India itself; (2) Indian colonization, with its vast cultural effects, was peaceful; it was not supported by precise political aims and was therefore far more acceptable than that of the Chinese, which was essentially political; (3) every crisis of Chinese power was accompanied by a re-emergence of autonomy in the states of Magna India; (4) in the protohistorical phase Magna India was connected with China (or rather with the continent), but with the establishment of Indian influence their relationship changed: this is the point at which the historical phase fully begins and the culture of India is set against the influence of China.[2]

The first information we have on the influence of Indian civilization in Magna India attests to the presence of Indianized states in a period going back at the latest to the second and third centuries A.D. In the case of Indochina we can speak in terms of the third century B.C., the period during which, according to tradition, Emperor Asoka sent two Buddhist monks, Sona and Uttara, to the "Land of Gold" (Suvarnabhūmi), usually identified as the ancient region of Mon in Burma. Sources mention two Indianized states: Lin-yi, the early state nucleus of ancient Champa, emerged in A.D. 192, in connection with the crisis of the Chinese empire that led to the fall of the Han dynasty; Funan, which included part of present-day Cambodia, on the lower course of the Mekong River, is said to have originated from the exploits of the Brahmin Kaundinya and from his marriage to a local princess. We are not presented with documented artistic manifestations until the sixth to eighth century A.D.; by this time, there is already a notable difference between constructions in Indochina and those in the Indonesian archipelago. The process of adaptation and modification must surely have been carried out in wood or other perishable materials, of which unfortunately no traces remain. However, the oldest architectural structures still in existence reveal close ties with their common source of inspiration, being all related to Indian religiosity and to the cult of kings who had been assimilated to divinities in the Buddhist or Hindu pantheons (in particular, the cult of Siva). This last aspect is proof that in the world of Magna India as well, architectural production was born of state initiative and connected with religious and royal values, the inspiration for which must be traced back to the Indian world, even though modified by local needs and tastes.

In general, it is not possible to trace the artistic development from any point in time earlier than the sixth century A.D. There are, however, regions for which this date must be moved ahead by at least four or six centuries.

*XVI. Java, Mount Ungaran, Temple
of the Cedong-sanga complex.*

193. a) Central Java, plain of Kedu, Candi Pawon; b) East Java, Panataram, so-called Dated Temple; c) Java, Duwur, access gate (candi bentar) (from Hallade, 1954).

194. Java, Dieng plateau, general view of the candis.
195. Java, Dieng plateau, Candi Puntedewa and Candi Sembadra.

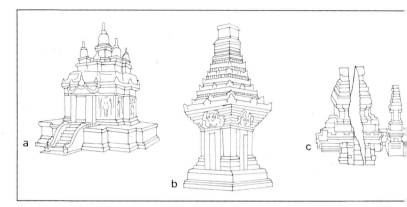

In Burma and Laos, for example, each lacking a strong political authority and the concomitant desire to construct buildings destined to endure, perishable materials were in use longer than in other areas. Any reconstruction of the architectural history of these regions is hampered by the disappearance of "lay" buildings, which must have constituted an integral part of local production, though there remains at best only epigraphic evidence of their existence. Equally important, the available documentation is rendered less meaningful by an underlying complexity of symbolism that often defies interpretation.

Indonesia

It is possible to follow the development of Indonesian architecture only from the eighth century on, the period during which the first stone monuments were built there. Nothing remains of the small wooden temples that in all probability were erected in earlier times, nor of the works in pressed brick ultimately destroyed by the region's tropical climate. Andesite, a type of volcanic rock, was the prime construction material, and sometimes stone temples were even demolished so that it could be reused.

Scholars in general distinguish between two cultural periods: the first, called either the Indo-Javanese or the Central Java period, spans the seventh to tenth centuries; the second, the East Java period, spans the eleventh to sixteenth centuries. In the central area of Java, Indo-Javanese culture reached its height under two rival dynasties. One was Buddhist, the Sailendra, and the other, the Mataram, was Saivite. A branch of the Sailendras is credited with the transformation of the kingdom of Sri Vijaya on the island of Sumatra into an empire. The East Java period witnessed a succession of three kingdoms and three dynasties, the last of which, the Madjapahit (1294-1520), extended its rule over other parts of the archipelago and exercised a strong influence on the development of Balinese culture. Buddhism and Saivism coexisted during this phase, merging in syncretic cults that are believed to have been imbued with mystical Tantrism. The conversion to Islam, beginning in the thirteenth century, was fully established on the coasts of Java and on the other islands by the fifteenth and sixteenth centuries.

We know very little about the foundations of Indonesian society in antiquity. It is clear, however, that the most important basic unit of economic and political life was the village, which was largely autonomous and had a mode of labor and production that served the needs of palace-cities and religious establishments and provided an active agricultural commerce. In general, we can assume that the social fabric of ancient Indonesia was largely made up of peasants and princes. Inscriptions going back to the eighth or ninth century, however, show that there was at that time a broad intermediate class consisting of a royal bureaucracy. Priests and monks presided over the sacred establishments (the temples and monasteries), and exercised exclusive control over the sources of revenue for the erection and maintenance of such buildings. The great ceremonies arranged for the king

196. Java, Dieng plateau, Candi Bima.

were attended by the village elders, who represented the people, and by groups of local merchants and artisans. We know almost nothing of the activities of these latter groups, which must also have included architects.[3]

It will be recalled that Indian penetration into Indonesia brought with it two religious systems: Brahmanism, especially in its Saivite aspect; and Buddhism, which after an initial appearance in its more simple Hinayana form, became widespread chiefly as the more broadly developed Mahayana, later to be mixed with the aforementioned Tantric elements. Saivism, probably because of its similarity to the autochthonous religious ideas of the Indonesians, appealed especially to the masses, while Buddhism remained the religion of the upper classes and court circles.

It can be assumed that a priestly elite, which initially must have been predominantly Indian, had direct and active access to the court. This elite was dedicated to the conversion of the Indonesian sovereigns, and the conversions they succeeded in motivating were total. It should not be forgotten that the sovereigns were in fact assimilated to the divinities of the new religions. On the other hand, this process of kingly deification, which found antecedents in the indigenous cult of dead chieftains, gave way to an actual faith that identified the royalty of the rulers with the will and protective capacities of the various Indian divinities.

The conception that we describe had, of course, important consequences in the sphere of art. For almost a millennium, major works of architecture and sculpture, commissioned by the monarchs themselves, were inspired by this particular vision. The architectural work became more and more charged with symbolic values, while departing from every functional aspect in the Western sense of the term.

Priests had particular importance in the construction of monuments: they persuaded the reigning monarch of their necessity and assumed the ensuing organizational burden. An inscription dating back to A.D. 778 makes clear this priestly role. Another inscription, dating back to 842, is equally enlightening. Not only were the priests required to be familiar with Indian treatises (*sāstras*), but some among them specialized as architects (*sthapatis*) or sculptors (*sthapakas*).[4]

From the stylistic standpoint, the Central Java period is the phase more strongly linked to Indian influences. Temple complexes show an ordered and symmetrical arrangement, whereas works of the East Java period are marked by a greater vertical thrust, an absence of monumental buildings, and a less ordered and less symmetrical arrangement. In our attempt to classify these structures, we may single out two fundamental types; the *candi* (the mausoleum or tomb temple), and the true shrine. The *candi*, despite its variations, conforms to a more or less fixed pattern, and is usually divided into three parts: a quadrangular base with moldings at top and bottom (one side being opened by a staircase whose width might vary); a cubic body, often with niches, and with a forepart on the same side as the staircase; the roof, divided into various levels, adorned with horseshoe niches, and with

198. *Java, Mount Ungaran, Temple No. 1 of the Cedong-sanga complex.*
199. *Java, Mount Ungaran, Temple No. 2 of the Cedong-sanga complex.*

200. *Java, Mount Ungaran, Temple No. 5 of the Cedong-sanga complex.*

miniature temples, with pinnacles or elements in the form of stupas, surmounted by a cylinder or truncated cone representing the lingam (phallus) of Siva. Inside the *candi*, in a pit dug before construction was begun, there was placed a casket containing the ashes of the sovereign or royal personage. In addition to being much reduced, the inner space had a purely symbolic importance. Among the oldest examples of this type of architecture, we might mention those on the Dieng plateau (ninth century), a center of the cult dedicated to Siva.

The most important monument, not only in Central Java but in all of Indonesia, is the stupa of Borobudur, whose construction goes back to the ninth century A.D. It is essentially a colossal stupa built around and over a small hill in the Kedu Valley. Even the choice of the site, like the form of the building, is symbolic, recalling Mount Meru (the mountain situated at the center of the universe) and the complex symbolism of "mountain" and "center." Borobudur is thus formed at its base by five terraces, approximately quadrangular but actually rather complex. The foundation was decorated with infernal scenes and then covered, since they were not intended to be seen. The first terrace constitutes the true base; the others diminish gradually in size as they ascend to the three last circular terraces, which represent a symbolic celestial plane and show a different kind of decoration. Centrally located on each of the four sides, and corresponding to the four cardinal points, are four staircases leading to the great bell-shaped *dagaba* placed at the top and at the geometric center of the construction. Each square terrace is defined by a wall, which serves as a baluster to the corridor of the terrace above. The walls and balusters are decorated with thirteen hundred reliefs recounting the last life on earth of Buddha (possibly inspired by the *Lalita Vistara*), episodes from his previous lives (*jātakas*), and pious legends (*avadānas*). The circular terraces, which have no walls or balusters, hold seventy-two bell-shaped stupas placed in concentric circles, but which differ from the crowning stupa in that they are pierced in such a way that in each the Dhyani Buddha inside is visible, if only partially. The more than four hundred niches, distributed on the square terraces and containing Dhyani Buddha images, are separated by stupas, each crowned by three other stupas. This whole series of small stupas imparts an elegantly animated outline to the entire construction.

The framing of the doors and niches displays the characteristic motif of the *kālā-makara* arch, a name that alludes to its combination of two stylized animal forms. The first, a terrifying lion's head, is carved on the upper part, while below, on the two sides of the opening or niche, we find aquatic monsters (*makaras*). The combination of these two elements recurs not only on arches but throughout Central Javanese architecture. Symbolically, they represent the two basic aspects of the cosmos—light and darkness, spirit and substance.

The significance of the Borobudur monument is still an open and much-discussed question. Some scholars consider it a place of meditation

201. Java, Borobudur, general view.   202, 203. Java, Borobudur, detail of   204. Java, plain of Kedu, Candi
the dagabas (bell-shaped stupas) on   Pawon, detail of the decoration.
the circular terraces.

205. *Java, plain of Kedu, Candi Pawon.*

206. *Java, plain of Kedu, Candi Mendut.*

207. *Java, plain of Prambanam, Loro Jongrang complex, temple in the southern court.*

208. *Java, plain of Prambanam, Loro Jongrang complex, Candi Siva.*

and edification for the worshiper, who by means of it ascends to the metaphysical level of the supreme Buddhas. It may, on the other hand, be a magical and religious symbol of the rule of dharma over the island and the universe. It has further been suggested that the construction may even be considered a colossal mausoleum.[5] It is even possible that the edifice, besides being a symbolic representation of the universe, is also a dynastic monument of the Sailendras, here seen as Bodhisattvas.

From an architectural standpoint, the three parts into which it is possible to divide Borobudur probably have a twofold symbolic significance: the three worlds (the infernal, natural, and celestial); and the three phases of the epiphany (manifestation) through which the unknowable reveals itself little by little in forms comprehensible to our spirit and perceptible to our senses. On the other hand, the association of a square structure as a symbol of the earth with a circular one as a symbol of the sky would make this work a true mandala. It is indeed a diagram (or psycho-cosmogram) through which the worshiper capable of meditating on and assimilating the value of the teachings expressed by the images proceeds, guided in his long journey until he achieves Enlightenment and salvation; it is not by chance that Borobudur is completely accessible all the way to the top. The edifying character of the work is, in any case, too obvious to be underestimated. The majesty of the monument reveals equally the extraordinary economic wealth of the ruling dynasty, with all the implications to be derived thereby.

As for non-Buddhist works, the most famous and esteemed of Indonesian Saivite temples is the Loro Jongrang complex on the plain of Prambanam. It was probably built between the middle of the ninth century and the beginning of the tenth by the Saivite dynasty descended from King Sañjaya. Reconstruction of the complex shows that it was originally divided into three parts. On one side of the central square three small temples face east; the central temple, dedicated to Siva, is flanked by two smaller ones celebrating Brahma and Vishnu. In front and parallel to each structure stand three lesser temples designed to honor the "vehicles" of the gods. Each temple rests on a square terrace enclosed by a baluster that forms a gallery. Two other temples, the smallest of all, are placed near the north and south gates.

In the reconstruction of which we speak, four rows of 156 shrines, probably votive constructions, are symmetrically laid out around the central area. It is believed that structures built of light materials (which have long since disappeared) and intended for monks, women dancers and pilgrims, were placed outside the encircling wall. It seems that the complex in its entirety was designed for the deification (in the form of Siva) of a king—perhaps Balitung of Mataram, as planned by his successor Daksa (A.D. 910-919). The reliefs that decorate the walls represent scenes from the *Rāmāyana*, and are thus erudite references to Indian culture.

In the second period, that of East Java, the arrangement of temple complexes is much less regular. The appearance of the shrines is altered more by a change in proportions, with a greater vertical development, than

210. *Java, plain of Prambanam,*
Candi Sewu complex, general view.

211. *Java, plain of Prambanam,*
Candi Sewu complex, one of the lesser
temples.

by any modification of architectural structures; we find here a transformation
of the entrance gates, which now are constituted by a false temple with a
pyramidal roof (candi bentar) vertically divided at the center. This division
allows for a short level corridor that passes between the two halves, and
permits entrance by a staircase also contained between the two parts. This
sectioning of the architectural structure clearly indicates that it was
appreciated for its volume of mass without any interest in the interior space.[6]
Furthermore, a taste for color and the picturesque becomes more developed,
with the appearance of painting and sometimes incrustations of ceramic in
the decoration of buildings.

None of the shrines of the East Java phase has the grandeur of major
Central Java monuments. This diminished interest in the magnificence of
architectural structures probably reflects a decline in economic possibilities
and a reduction in the labor force.

Very little remains of the period of the Singhasari dynasty. We might
mention the "bath" at Belahan, probably the sovereign's funeral monument,
dated A.D. 1049 and attributed to the reign of King Airlangga, and the royal
tombs of Gunung Kawi on Bali, which take the form of candis dug out of
the tufa. The new Indonesian architectural vision was expressed in such
works as Candi Saventar and Candi Kidal (thirteenth century), and
particularly in the Saivite complex at Panataram; (fourteenth to fifteenth
centuries), which clearly manifests the cultural power of the Madjapahit
Kingdom. Generally thought to be a state temple (which is doubtful), it
is distinguished by its agitated and asymmetrical plan. Important structures
in this complex are the Temple of the Nagas (the name refers to serpent
gods symbolizing water) and Candi Siva, the so-called Dated Temple of
1369, whose pyramidal roof appears to be supported by the large grotesque
masks of kālās placed above the doors.

214. *Java, plain of Prambanam, Candi Sari.*

The fall of the Madjapahit Kingdom in the second half of the fifteenth century marks the beginning of the Islamic period in Indonesia. The decline of Indian culture in this region now begins, at least as far as architecture is concerned. Only the island of Bali would preserve intact the pre-Islamic Hindu culture for any length of time.

Cambodia (the Khmers)

The most important Indianized state in ancient Indochina was Funan, situated in Cochin China between the Bassac River and the Gulf of Siam. In addition to the legends relating to its birth and to the "Land of Gold," certain Chinese sources dating from about the third century A.D. speak of its great wealth in gold, silver, pearls, and spices. Archaeological aerial reconnaissance of these areas has revealed the existence of a dense network of canals, interconnected and laid out in a predominantly northeast-southwest direction. The purpose of these canals was to drain the floodwaters of the Bassac to the sea and "wash" the soil otherwise made saline by drought, thus permitting an intensive cultivation of rice, and to shelter an imposing river fleet. Along the vital points of this canal system traces of cities have been discerned, in which the canals penetrated, dividing them into quarters. This extraordinary complex testifies to the existence of a remarkable economic and political power.[7]

Unfortunately, almost nothing remains of the architecture of the period; the houses must have been built on wooden piles. Durable materials were apparently reserved for shrines, of which there remain only a few vestiges that defy firm identification. What little remains, however, bespeaks a strong Indian influence, though we also find among them some Chinese and Roman objects.

During the same period, there arose in the middle Mekong Basin another Indianized state, also known by the name given it by the Chinese sources—Chen-la. It existed as early as the sixth century, and inscriptions going back to the seventh and eighth centuries testify to the presence in Chen-la of people of Khmer origin. The progressive expansion of Chen-la brought about the almost total conquest of Funan at the beginning of the eighth century. Isanavarman, the king of Chen-la (A.D. 616-635), founded a new capital, Isanapura (today Sambor Prei Kuk), from which the early art of Chen-la—or rather, the first phase of Khmer art—takes its name, the Sambor style.

In this case as well, aerial reliefs allow us to reconstruct the system of urbanization and exploitation of natural space in Chen-la. Its cities were vast expanses of terrain surrounded by earth walls and by a trench that drew water from a permanent waterway; when filled with water, the trench provided irrigation for the rice fields within the enclosure. This technique for supplying water was brought to Cambodia by the Khmers. Though profoundly different from that of Funan, it required from the beginning a centralized society and a single strong authority—precisely the one that was

161

217. East Java, Blitar, Panataram, Temple of the Nagas.

218. East Java, Blitar, Panataram, view of the complex.

219. East Java, Malang, Candi Jago.

163

220. *East Java, Blitar, Panataram,*
Candi Siva, or the so-called Dated
Temple.

221. *East Java, Malang, Candi*
Kidal.

222. *East Java, Malang, Candi*
Singhasari.

223. Plans of temples at Angkor:
a) Phimai; b) Banteay Samre (from
Boisselier, 1966).

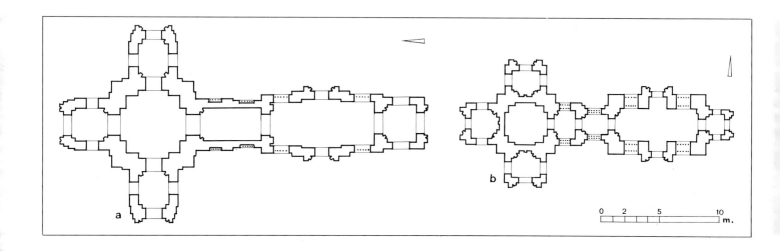

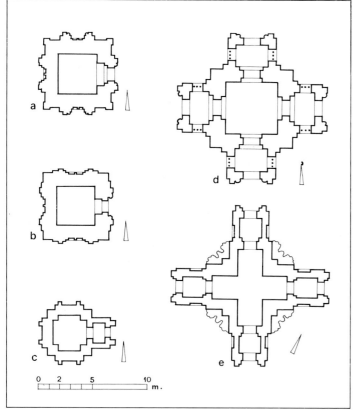

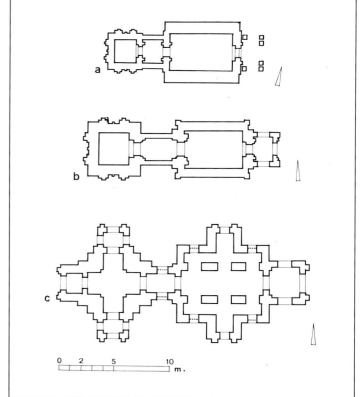

224. *Plans of temples at Angkor:*
a) Bakong; b) Baksei Chamrong;
c) Mangalartha; d) Ta Keo; e) preah
Thkol (from Boisselier, 1966).

225. *Plans of temples at Angkor:*
a) prasat *(tower-sanctuary), Thom of*
Koh Ker; b) prasat, *Sek Ta Tuy;*
c) Wat Ek (from Boisselier, 1966).

226. *Phnom Bakheng, aerial view of the temple.*

227. *Banteay Srei, elevation, section, and plan of the southern tower-sanctuary (from Boisselier, 1966).*

228. *a) Temple of Prah Ko,* prasat; *b) Banteay Srei, entrance hall to the central tower-sanctuary (from Hallade, 1954).*

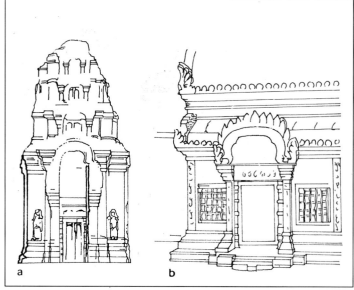

a   b

to develop into the structure of Angkor.

The architecture was substantially religious; only inscriptions testify to the existence of lay works of public utility, such as hospitals and "houses with fire" (designed to shelter travelers), all of which were constructed of perishable materials and are now totally destroyed.

The Khmers, like the Indians before them, conceived the temple not as a meeting place for the faithful but as the home of the god it honored; they believed he actually lived there in the form of his sacred image. The Khmer temple was therefore relatively small. The structures of shrines included a tower (*prasat*) for the principal deity and one or more towers for the god's spouse and his "vehicle." Secondary constructions, designed to preserve cult objects and everything connected with the liturgy and exegesis, were added to these buildings. A wall with doors enclosed the complex, and inside a second wall were constructions in perishable materials—the dwellings for priests, musicians, and male and female dancers.

The temples gave concrete form to, and symbolically expressed, the religious beliefs of the country. The sacred building appears rigorously centered and oriented according to the four cardinal points; the façade and principal entrance faced east, the source of life. The main sanctuary was the image of Mount Meru, center of the world, on which the deity has his seat. It was built at the center of the city, close to the palace of the king, who held a mandate on earth from the gods. This organization and arrangement were to remain almost unaltered in the course of the centuries and throughout the changing styles; the static quality of a metaphysical type of

229. *Banteay Srei, northern library of the sanctuary, exterior.*

230. *Banteay Srei, entrance gate (gopura) to the sanctuary.*

169

structure hindered any fundamental alterations. On the religious level, such repetition is not a sign of weakness, but has the significance of a holy rite. This instinct of preservation is also reflected in the persistence, in stone constructions, of building structures and systems much more suitable for wood—the material that had been used for older buildings.

The grandeur of monuments is generally more evident in periods of peace and equilibrium. We owe, for example, the two architectural complexes of Sambor Prei Kuk—one to the north, the other to the south—to the powerful reign of Isanavarman. Nevertheless, under his successor and during a less tranquil time, the Prei Kmeng style flourished. It is a style characterized by sanctuary-towers that are of scant value. Although there was during this period a progressive and strong affirmation of Hinduism, the use of Mahayana Buddhist images spread remarkably. Chen-la found itself in troubled times during the entire eighth century. Only when a new equilibrium was created, coinciding with the founding of Angkor, would they be resolved.

Architecture, as well as sculpture, became impoverished and there ensued an unfortunate period of obvious decline. It was, however, more a political and social crisis than a cultural one; evidently the economy reacted negatively to the interruption of trade relations with India. A new political organization had to be created, as well as a new social and economic one, in order for these arts to be revitalized.

It is probable that the influence of Indonesia, then ruled by the Sailendras, contributed to this rebirth. At that time, the Javanese dynasty exercised a right of sovereignty over the South China Sea and in particular over the coasts of Malaysia, where Mahayana Buddhism was widespread. On the other hand, on the political level, the Sailendras offered Chen-la the example of a great civilization of a monarchical character. It is thought that Jayavarman II, who restored equilibrium and founded the Khmer Empire, spent a long time, either voluntarily or as a hostage, at the court of Java. Upon his return to Cambodia about A.D. 790, he prepared to reorganize the territory of Chen-la by founding a series of capitals, of which the most important was Mahendraparvata. Here he had a lingam built as a symbol of the god Siva and of his own royal divinity; from that point on this would be the emblem of all succeeding Khmer kings. In this way Jayavarman and his successors asserted themselves as universal sovereigns, legitimizing their power by a direct relation to the deity, which in its turn was the essence, order, and mover of the universe. The Khmer territory was again united under a central authority. This political and social order was accompanied by the achievement of a vigorous art, which found expression in a succession of various styles and in imposing architectural monuments.

An innovation of tremendous importance to the establishment of Khmer power on the political and economic level can be attributed to Indravarman (A.D. 877-889). At Roluos, his residence, this ruler supervised the construction of an admirable hydraulic system that helped to ensure three

171

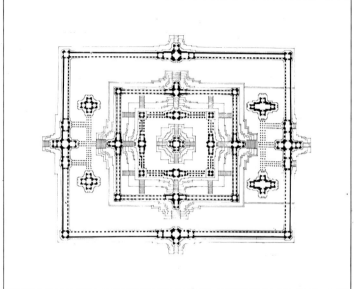

centuries of extraordinary prosperity for the country. The first step undertaken was the construction of the artificial lake (*barai*) known as Indrataka, which distributed water to the rice fields by means of a network of irrigation canals. The water was then conveyed to the trenches that served the city and defined its boundaries. River navigation, which among other things facilitated the transporting of construction materials, was now possible along the canals. B.P. Groslier has defined the meaning of the innovation and its value to the local economy: "In this way the Angkor city is no longer a simple assemblage of its inhabitants around the temple of the god who protects them. It is the fulcrum of a rational system of soil cultivation, utilizing natural resources in the best manner, and, depending on the case, integrating and replacing them."[8]

The effectiveness of this system, in an area where the fundamental problem remained that of drought, is confirmed by the creation of identical structures in the centuries that followed. Even when, as a result of dynastic conflicts, the Khmer kings abandoned Angkor and moved to Koh Ker, they prepared for settlement in an arid area by setting up a hydraulic system similar to that of Angkor.

It is obvious that it was possible to carry out undertakings of this kind only in an exceptionally strong centralized state, and that the success of these hydraulic systems conferred an almost magical power on the king who constructed one. By providing water in this manner, he gave life. The divinity of the rulers, as well as the veneration bestowed on them when dead,

XVII. Java, Borobudur, detail.

237. *Angkor Wat, plan of the temple complex (from Groslier, 1961).*
238. *Angkor Wat, central gallery of the galleries in Greek-cross form (from Boisselier, 1966).*

239. *Angkor Wat, northwest library of the third city wall, plan (from Boisselier, 1966).*

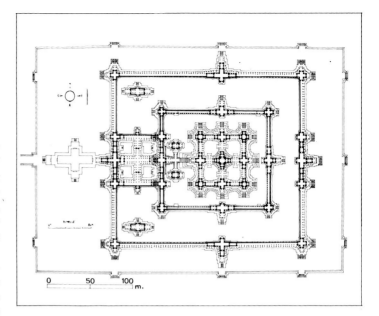

was thus legitimized in the socio-economic sphere. This fundamental view would remain a constant in the sequence of Khmer art. A succession of various styles ensued, with names that derive from the most important centers of the period to which they belong. An examination of the more significant monuments will indicate the basic architectural types of each. An interesting aspect of our study will be the Khmers' admirable use of their network of canals in the construction of shrines by arranging buildings against a background of water in an artistic way.

The basic architectural types used by the Khmers were the tower-sanctuary (*prasat*) and the temple-mountain; the gallery was added later. The more imposing works were constituted by the varied composition of these three elements. The *prasat* is square in plan and built of brick. It opens toward the east, and is surmounted by a roof of superimposed levels that reproduces, on a progressively diminishing scale, the structure of the main body. The temple-mountain is a construction formed by a terraced pyramid (the number of terraces would vary with time), crowned at the top by five *prasats*, placed quincuncially. This basic structure would be enhanced by the addition of a series of sandstone towers onto the individual terraces.

Both types can be observed in the Khmer architecture of the early style, known as Kulen (eighth to ninth centuries), which at Ak Yom offers our first example of the temple-mountain in its simplest form. The Bakheng style provides other fine examples of the temple-mountain in the pyramid at Bakong and in the complex at Phnom Bakheng constructed at the end of the ninth century. Compared to the Ak Yom temple, the one at Bakong has a more complicated structure, with a greater number of terraces and towers on the individual levels. Furthermore, the site is enclosed by two successive stone walls that alternate with two wide moats. The Phnom Bakheng complex, in its rich symbology, is an actual calendar in stone, indicating on its various horizons the positions and phases of the planets. Along with the temple-mountain, use of the tower-sanctuary continues: the Phnom Krom and the Phnom Bok are each formed by three aligned towers constructed entirely of stone.

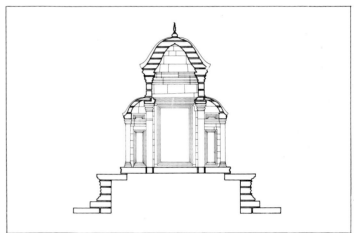

Following the era during which Koh Ker was the capital, it was Rajendravarman who initiated the return to Angkor (A.D. 944-968). The tradition of the temple-mountain continued, but other sanctuaries of more modest dimensions were built by the chief vassals of the king. Among these we might mention the Saivite temple of Banteay Srei, consecrated by the Brahmin Yainavaraha. The temple, formed by three concentric enclosures, includes three tower-sanctuaries aligned on a terrace. The east gate of the main temple is preceded by a vaulted forepart in brick, while libraries and long halls surround the complex. The forms and proportions that character-ize this construction—scarcely verticalized due to a particular wish to achieve balanced effects—are especially elegant and harmonious.

There followed a politically unsettled period during which the Khmers failed to initiate any notable variations in the artistic field. The temple-

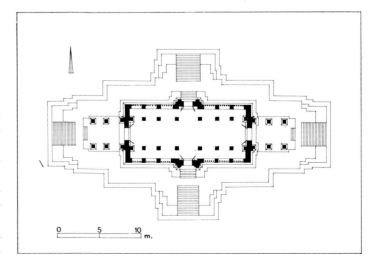

240. *Angkor Wat, southern side of the second gallery.*

241. *Angkor Wat, axial view of the western part.*

242. *Angkor Wat, aerial view.*

245. Angkor Thom, plan of the Bayon (from Groslier, 1961).

246. Angkor Thom, central sanctuary of the Bayon, plan (from Boisselier, 1966).

247. Angkor, Baksei Chamrong (from Hallade, 1954).

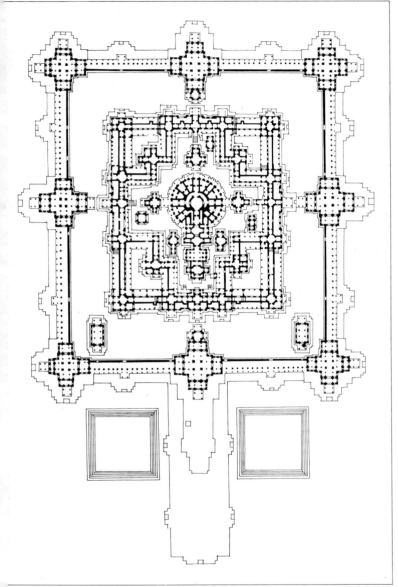

0   2   6   12
                   m.

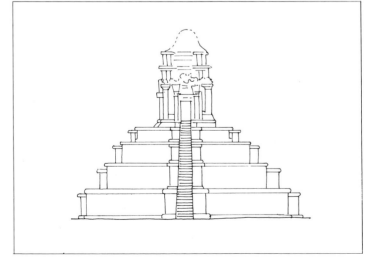

248. Angkor Thom, aerial view of the Bayon.

mountain did not acquire its definitive form until the construction of the Ta Keo around A.D. 1000, which marked the culmination of a development begun as early as Ak Yom.

The entire five-level pyramid of Ta Keo is covered in stone. On the highest terrace, its innovators placed quincuncially five sandstone towers. Around the second level there runs a gallery, which is accentuated at its four corners by roughly constructed towers and enlivened at the center of each side by an access pavilion.

Later builders of the temple-mountain (like those at Baphuon) would emphasize the development of such galleries and erect towers at the corners. The *prasat* of this period, also built of stone, rests on a platform and is sometimes preceded by a forepart. To the sides of the main entrance, we often find libraries. Surrounded by moats and ponds, these sanctuaries, even in their reduced size, have the same quality of refinement as the more imposing monuments.

The fame of Khmer art is largely connected with the Angkor Wat complex, the temple-mountain of Suryavarman II (A.D. 1113-1150). This temple, whose main façade looks west, is bounded by a trench that received water from Siemréap via a canal. A road flanked by balusters adorned with serpent motifs leads to the main gate of an enclosure that reproduces on a reduced scale the façade of the temple. The central tower has two lateral wings of galleries; they terminate in a smaller tower. The columns that support the galleries are reflected in the water. Within the enclosure rises the temple, a pyramid with three superimposed terraces, each surrounded by a gallery enhanced by towers and pavilions. Three staircases on the western side lead to three more galleries supported by pillars, and then above to the three staircases of the second terrace. The edifice is constructed in accordance with an extraordinary perspective composition: the height of each of the three terraces seems slowly to increase as one ascends, and each terrace shifts, progressively drawn back, so that the structure as a whole does not give the impression of being inclined toward the spectator about to ascend it.

Angkor Wat is flanked by a series of identical shrines whose plan and structural elements differ from the central complex only in that they are developed horizontally.

The last great creations of Khmer art took place under Jayavarman VII (A.D. 1181-1220), whose powerful motivation and strength of purpose arrested for a time a decadence that later proved to be inevitable. Incongruously, this enigmatic ruler was especially cruel to his enemies, yet was at the same time a deeply religious man. Converted to Mahayana Buddhism, he adopted a new concept with regard to the deified sovereign. In his forty-year reign he devoted particular attention to the ancestor cult, restored almost all the ancient temples, and initiated and dedicated to himself a great number of works, often insisting on changes in the original plans during their construction.

249. Angkor Thom, southern gate and access road of the Bayon.

250. *Angkor Thom, view of the central mass of the Bayon.*

251. *Angkor Thom, southern gate, detail of the upper part.*

254. a) Nhatrang (Vietnam), main tower of the Po Nagar temple; b) Binh Dinh, Towers of Silver, detail of a kalan (tower-sanctuary); c) Mi-son A 1 (Vietnam), detail of a temple door (from Hallade, 1954).

a

b

c

By following this course, Jayavarman VII made Angkor Thom truly his capital, and at its center built his towering temple-mountain, the Bayon. He actually succeeded, with the help of the men he appointed to carry out the work, in surpassing the complex and refined symbolism with which this type of monument had long been charged.

The original plan of the Bayon was modified and made more complicated in the course of construction. The initial layout included a vaulted gallery in the form of a Greek cross. Its corners, however, were later closed off by a gallery set at right angles, and the whole was enclosed by still another gallery. At the center of the inner gallery, and on a large base, there stood the sanctuary, circular in plan. Its central chapel was complemented by as many as twelve radial chapels. Each tower was built over the chapels and pavilions and was carved with four faces symbolizing the gaze of the Compassionate Buddha that pervades the universe, placed toward the four cardinal points. The central sanctuary housed a statue of Buddha in meditation, and the radial chapels contained images representing great dignitaries. The colossal faces on the towers served to identify the ruler with divinity and referred as well to the universal sovereignty (a theoretical and wise sovereignty) of the deified king, who looks in all directions and watches over the country, which is represented below by the figures of powerful court dignitaries.

With the death of Jayavarman VII, the process of decadence was accelerated; with him died the last god-king. The world of the Khmers survived only until 1430. Progressive decay of the central power brought about a collapse of the economy and with the disappearance of this central authority, the land that had been wrenched from the desert became arid once again. The devastating attacks of the Thais gave the death blow to a territory that by now was well in decline.

The art that had been inspired by the monarchy and the cult of the king decayed, and the use of perishable materials resumed. It was the sad destiny of the works that followed to have no value beyond that of the historical moment.

Champa

We find that, beginning in the third century A.D., Champa is often mentioned in the Chinese texts, which refer to it as Lin-yi. They describe the ancient kingdom, in direct contact with the Han colonies in Tonkin, as a land formed by warrior states inhabited by the Chams. This was a population of highly expert navigators who, living in a coastal forest area rich in spices, established early connections with Indian traders. The region was later divided into kingdoms or principalities: the most important of these in the beginning were Amaravati, today Quang Nam; Vijaya, today Binh Dinh; Kauthara, on the plain of Nhatrang; and Panduranga, on the plain of Phanrang.

Close relations with Funan, and diplomatic ties and wars with China,

brought about a political situation favorable to penetration by both Indian
and Chinese influences. We know that at the beginning of the fifth century
the sovereign Bhadravarman founded a sanctuary dedicated to Siva in the
mountain cirque of Mi-son. Chinese sources note also that the Chams were
already masters of brick construction. A more direct knowledge of their art
is not available, however, until the seventh century. It appears that after a
series of bloody struggles, the Cham Kingdom established friendly relations
with Indonesia, an entente that is reflected in the style of the Duong Dong
complex (ninth century A.D.). Following some conflict with the Khmers,
whose influence is clearly apparent in the style of Mi-son, a very grave threat
to the Chams was posed by the hostile expansion of ancient Annam, which
had become independent. In A.D. 982 the Annamese succeeded in seizing
the capital, and the Chams were forced to withdraw to Vijaya, which
remained the center of the country even when, for a certain time, the
northern provinces were reconquered.

Persistent Vietnamese pressure, if only with sporadic thrusts in the nature
of incursions, had to be dealt with at the same time the country was
threatened by the Khmers. In 1145, after fifty years of relative calm, the
dynasty and country were overwhelmed by the Khmer armies. The war,
which lasted a hundred years, weakened both adversaries to the advantage
of the Thais and Vietnamese. In 1417, even the name of Champa disappears;
the territory was completely assimilated by the Vietnamese.

Cham art differs profoundly from that of the Khmers, despite their
common Indian model and reciprocal exchanges and influences. This
difference is not a question of a natural diversity in taste, produced by diverse
cultures and sensibilities, but is rather the result of aesthetic conceptions that
diverge because of the radically different functions that the two kingdoms
attributed to art.

The essential reason for this divergence is to be sought in the Cham
socio-political structure. The system, founded on the division of land, kept
the country constantly divided into principalities. Sometimes they were held
together by a particularly energetic king, but never with the slightest
possibility of reducing his realm to a socially and economically centralized
state. Art thus remained the privilege of kings, and had only the dimensions
of their power.[9]

Even though—like the Khmers, and perhaps due to Indonesian influence—the Cham kings adopted the cult of the deified king, they never
created a temple-mountain, nor any great complexes that can even remotely
be compared to those of Angkor. In any case, the Chams' sense of space
was not that of the Khmers. Cham architecture possesses no large complexes,
with the exception of the Mahayana monastery at Duong Dong. Cham
temple structures are constituted only by the grouping of a few sanctuaries,
square in plan and enclosed by a wall. At times (but this is rather rare)
sanctuaries are preceded by a long hall. In practice, we can say that the only
type of building used in Cham architecture is the tower-sanctuary known

189

as the *kalan*, square in plan and always constructed of brick.

The basic structure of the *kalan* is that of a cubic mass topped by a roof of several superimposed levels that tends to become narrower toward the top, imparting to the whole a considerable vertical thrust. Through a succession of stylistic variations, this thrust was to become more accentuated, due not only to the attenuation of the base (no longer cubic) toward the top, but also to the formation of high socle beneath the base itself; and finally, as a visual effect, to the presence of decorative elements, sometimes strongly projecting, that help to emphasize the vertical effect.

Inside the *kalan*, the covering of the cell is also raised, assuming the form of a fireplace chimney. Of particular importance is the outer decoration, consisting of moldings, fixed (especially plant-form) motifs, and architectural elements. We find, for example, false pillars, often in pairs, or projecting arches of various kinds, but always devoid of any static function. The decoration is always more profuse and elaborate at the lower part of the building.

The roof of the structure consists, as already mentioned, of diminishing planes, which often display at their corners miniature replicas of the building, sculptured in the round. In many cases, it is actually the levels themselves in their entirety that appear as reduced copies of the building below. Diminishing toward the top, in ever smaller forms, they impart to the building a strange effect of flight toward the sky.

Each of the four sides of the parallelepiped of the base has a door (sometimes two of them are false), flanked by small columns and surmounted by a polylobate arch with a characteristically flowing outline. The admirable attention to proportions and the type of decoration itself help to give the *kalan* a particular effect of energy and harmony that constitutes its principal charm.

We are faced here, of course, with only a single type of construction that furthermore remained substantially unaltered. Yet it is possible to follow the development of the *kalan*, for it is marked by a progressive change in its forms, especially the decoration of the arches over the doors and niches. Initially, in the Hoa-lai style of about the ninth century, the arches appear in the form of an inverted U, rising and enlivened by means of a polylobate contour. In the Duong Dong style that marked the third quarter of the ninth century, the arch is decorated by a central flower from which masses of plants fall to the sides, forming rosettes along the entire curve; the garland under the cornice is enriched by ornamental foliage. Such is the case of the main tower of the Duong Dong complex, the great Mahayana Buddhist monastery founded in A.D. 875 by Indravarman II and dedicated to Avalokitesvara, the Bodhisattva of the Compassionate Gaze. Inside the Duong Dong enclosure, whose perimeter is almost a kilometer in length, rises an ensemble of brick constructions, placed in a space divided into successive courtyards oriented along an east-west transverse axis. In the first courtyard, which is the last for the worshiper entering from the eastern side,

there are eighteen shrines. On the middle axis, surrounded by other sanctuaries, rises the central tower, open on four sides and containing an altar that no doubt once bore Avalokitesvara's statue, which has since disappeared.

The next style, called Mi-son A 1, marks the abandonment of the excessive development of plant-form decorations and the return to a simpler and more balanced composition (ninth century). The central tower, characteristically Mi-son A 1, develops its own structure vertically, reduces the superstructures, and introduces more slender pillars devoid of decoration (five in number). The curvature of its arches tends to disappear and be replaced by a linear structure, which may be inscribed in an equilateral triangle. At the corners of the tower rise the typical sandstone spires, a salient feature of Cham monuments.

A time of transition, corresponding politically to the period of Khmer domination, followed the period during which this elegant and harmonious art was created. Then, at the beginning of the twelfth century, the so-called Binh Dinh style developed, in which the *kalan* ultimately becomes primarily a geometric mass, a parallelepiped with light moldings. Arches assume a lanceolate form, and superstructures are multiplied, repeating the structure of the building. They are, however, reduced in height to endow the *kalan* with a continuous curve in its skyline, imitating the ogival contour typical of the towers of Angkor. It is very likely that the construction of such famous works as the Towers of Copper and Towers of Gold goes back to the end of the thirteenth century. Projecting supplementary arches were later added to the principal arches, some superstructures were multiplied but without any explicit criterion, and corner motifs were stylized to the point of becoming stone hooks. The garland under the cornice disappeared, often to be replaced by zoomorphic friezes.

After the fourteenth century, with the dismemberment of their country, the art of the Chams inevitably declined. Finally, it exhausted itself in the repetitive aridity that marks such works of the period as the *kalan* at Po Romé, which is formed by a cumbersome complex of four brick structures, awkwardly constructed and decorated with heavy and illogical niches.

Burma

The art of Burma reflects more than any other in Indochina the cultural influence of the Indian world. The first certain evidence of this Indianization appears in fifth - to - sixth century fragments of gold leaf on which sacred Buddhist texts are incised in the Pali language. The Indians, however, also introduced Hinduism into Burma along with Mahayana and Hinayana Buddhism. Only the latter religious form would maintain a position of importance in the history of this region.

The earliest populations of the area, those whom we might theoretically consider autochthonous, were probably Mons and Pyus of Mongolian stock. In the ninth century, however, groups of people of Tibetan origin emigrated

258. *Prome (outskirts), stupa of Bawbawgyi.*

259. *Prome (outskirts), temple of Bebegyi.*

260. Prome (outskirts), temple of Lemyethna.

264. Pagan, temple of Nat Hlaung Gyaung.
265. Pagan, stupa of Ngakywendaung.
266. Pagan, temple of Ananda, elevation and section (from Griswold, 1963).
267. Pagan, temple of Ananda.

south from their original lands along the borders of Tibet and China and entered northern Burma, where they took control of two regions: Kyaukse, economically important for its abundant rice production; and Pagan, a key region because of such attributes as a strategic position, a natural road network, and commercial possibilities. Under Anawratha (A.D. 1044-1077), the Burmese were converted to Hinayana Buddhism and extended their rule to include most of the country. Anawratha's capital city of Pagan, where Mon prisoners captured during the invasion were concentrated, became, also because of their presence, a center for the spread of Buddhism, and it was here, during the reign of Kyanzittha (A.D. 1084-1112), that the great building period began. The tolerance of the new king permitted the coexistence of different religions, and under his successor a truly Burmese style began that was destined to triumph for two centuries. Extremely friendly relations were established with Ceylon, and it was perhaps in this period that Tantric Buddhism arrived in Pagan. In 1287 Burma was invaded by the Mongols, who under the leadership of Kublai Khan seized the capital and ended the Burmese dynasty. Not until the fifteenth and sixteenth centuries, when political conditions were more favorable and new dynasties arose, were there signs of a rebirth and encouragement of the arts.

An exhaustive study of Burmese art and architecture, one that would enable us to follow their development over the centuries and attempt a classification by styles and schools, has yet to be made. Of civil architecture, nothing remains. Numerous monuments of a religious nature survive, however, although they are often in a considerable state of ruin due to war, pillage, and careless restoration. Fortunately, the dry climate of the area has helped to preserve a much greater number of works than in any other part of Southeast Asia. Except for a few Hindu constructions and some others deriving from Mahayana Buddhism, all the monuments of this period were inspired by the Hinayana Buddhism of the Theravadin sect (whose stronghold was in Ceylon). Since it is not possible to trace the artistic phenomenology of this region with sufficient certainty, we will proceed by examining construction techniques and the various types of buildings.

A typical feature of architectural construction is the use of rib vaults, obtained by the close positioning of flattened arches, which may be erected without centering by utilizing a connecting element. The question of whether this building system originated in India or China is still to be resolved.[10] The material employed, except for certain small works built of stone, is generally brick, covered by thick stucco in which decoration was incised. Colored tablets of enameled terracotta were often used for decoration; or, inside the monuments, carved wooden panels. Stupas and sanctuaries remained massive in appearance, with interior spaces looking as though they had been excavated from the rock. The Indian technique of cut or excavated architecture left traces even in the constructed architecture of a foreign country.

Specialists have followed different systems in the classification of

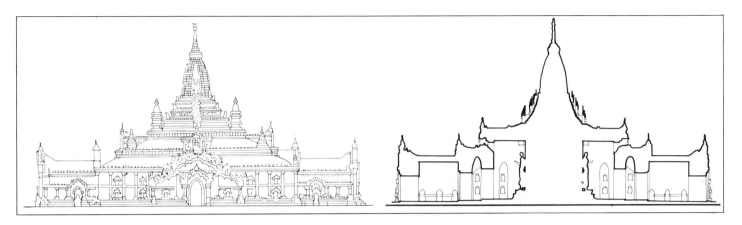

XXIV. Bangkok, Wat P'ra Keo,
courtyard of the Royal Chapel of the
Emerald Buddha.

269. Pagan, temple of Mahabodhi.

272. *Sajjanalaya, Wat Cetiya Jet Teo.*
273. *Sajjanalaya, Wat Chang Lom.*

Burmese buildings. Some distinguish ten types of monuments (De Beylié); others, nine (U Lu Pe Win); still others indicate only two types as being fundamental. They are the stupa and the building that includes a hall for the cult or habitation; the others are considered to be simple variations of these basic types (Parmentier and Marchal).[11] We will follow this last criterion, examining particularly those types and subtypes of which important examples survive.

Traditionally, the Burmese stupa is composed of four parts: (1) a masonry terrace, square in plan; (2) a very high plinth, by preference polygonal in plan; (3) the bell-shaped body of the actual stupa, ending in (4) a conical spire—often formed by rings—crowned by a parasol (*hti*). Variations are infinite. Hemispherical domes are rare, and are always flared at the bottom so as to introduce the bell shape; cylindrical bodies that replace the polygonal form of the so-called plinth are more frequent. There are even conical stupas, knob-shaped structures with concave contours that result from a widening at the base, and bulb-shaped ones.

The Burmese bell-shaped stupa, especially frequent in Pagan, can be a very elaborate architectural type. The terrace, which is square, has in these cases superimposed levels that diminish toward the top and act as ambulatories. At the four cardinal points, staircases connected by ramps permit passage from one level to another. The body of the bell-shaped stupa rises directly from the highest level of the base. In addition, there are enough other, equally complicated, forms to justify the more elaborate classification systems of which we spoke.

However, the Burmese stupa does display two characteristics that distinguish it from the Indian structure: (1) the absence of a terrace with baluster (*harmikā*) surmounting the dome from which the spire rises; (2) a greater development of the base, composed, as we have mentioned, of superimposed square platforms that constitute a kind of ambulatory to which one ascends by means of axial stairs. Furthermore, the Burmese stupa tends toward progressive verticality. The form of the older stupas can be cylindrical, like the Bawbawgyi of the seventh century near Prome, or, like the Payama and Payagyi, be shaped like a giant sugar loaf. The Pagan dynasty preferred the bell-shaped form, which perhaps brought with it certain Singhalese components, whose number has still not been satisfactorily determined.

The latest Pagan edifice that we know of is the stupa of Mingalazedi, begun in 1274. The construction is formed by three terraces surmounted by a stupa with a molded circular base; it is topped by a bell-shaped drum ending in a conical spire. False *kalasas* (vases for ambrosia) are placed at the corners of the terraces, while at the four corners of the level from which the actual stupa rises there are four small stupas that reproduce in miniature the structure of the central one. At the center of the four sides of the terraces, staircases lead to the upper levels. This monument at Mingalazedi is the most characteristic Burmese stupa. The type of building with an inner hall, very

widespread at least until the Pagan period, offers various subtypes, though it always has the appearance of a compact mass of bricks in which chapels and corridors have been dug out. Buildings of this type are generally known as cave-buildings. A vaulted cell opens at the center of the mass, and over it is raised a block that supports an imposing crown of the sikhara type.

The most important monuments of this kind are the Ananda, consecrated in A.D. 1091, and the Thatbyinnyu (A.D. 1144). The Ananda, built by King Kyanzittha (A.D. 1084-1112), marks the triumph of the style known as Mon. According to legend, this sanctuary was intended to reproduce the form of the cave of Nandamula, where Indian monks who had been received at the Burmese court had once lived.

The plan of the construction is that of a Greek cross. In it the arms are formed by massive porticoes placed around the central square. The latter consists of an immense and solid block of brick that rises to support the tower structure, which is modeled after a sikhara and thus gives the building its religious significance. The two narrow concentric corridors inside enable the worshiper to perform a circumambulation around the 30-foot statues of Buddha, placed in niches on the four walls of the central block. The outer roof is formed by a series of diminishing platforms, from the last of which rises the cupola-tower. The corners of the platforms bear repetitions, on a reduced scale, of the central dome.

The Thatbyinnyu, built in Pagan in A.D. 1144 by King Alaungsithu, is similar to the Ananda. It does not, however, possess the four wings that give the latter its cruciform structure. The square plan is very obvious, and the central construction constitutes a dado around which an enormous basic mass is developed, similar in various ways to the base of the Ananda. The shape of the monument can best be described as a stupa that by its base terraces rises on a wide platform in the form of a cube, which in its turn is supported by enormous base terraces. In all, the monument includes five levels, of which the highest is crowned by the sikhara, while the two immediately below it form a kind of vihara.

Siam (Thailand)

The actual history of Siam begins only in the thirteenth century, when the Thais of the middle Menam Basin succeeded in freeing themselves from Khmer domination and founding their first kingdom, at Sukhodaya. Archaeological evidence nevertheless enables us partially to reconstruct the previous period as well, which is of no small importance for the formation of Siamese art and civilization.

It would appear that at least as early as the sixth century A.D. there existed in the Menam Delta an Indianized state, Dvaravati. The bronze images of Buddha created by Dvaravati artists (discovered at Korat and Nagara Pathama) show in fact a clear Indian influence of the Gupta period. It is probable that the expansion of this kingdom is related to the dismemberment of Funan, but though we can reconstruct the historical situation little is

known of Siam's artistic development in this period.

Later, in the ninth to tenth centuries, the country underwent a process of progressive "Khmerization" (in the sense of an absolute hegemony of Khmer culture at the expense of local traditions), which reached its height in the eleventh century, when Suryavarman I, a Siamese Mon, ascended the Khmer throne to become one of the greatest rulers of this multinational empire. However, despite the preponderant Khmer influence, Siam remained the most orthodox center of Hinayana Buddhism, which was so strong a faith that it asserted itself even at Angkor when the conquests of the Khmer kings led to the integration of Siamese territory with their other possessions. Unfortunately, we know very little of the art of this period (eleventh to twelfth centuries) as well, aside from the undeniable fact that it was an art inspired by Buddhism. Only recently has research in the vicinity of Nakhon Pathom (Nagara Pathama) brought to light the remains of a few large brick complexes.

In the architectural sphere, the existence of stupas of obvious Indian derivation has been ascertained, as well as that of a kind of reliquary-monument or chaitya, consisting of a brick cube surmounted by a full roof with molded levels. Chaityas were decorated on the outside by Buddhist images under arcades, and temple complexes were surrounded by ambulatory galleries. Often the chaityas were erected on imposing terraces. The two most interesting monuments of this kind are Wat P'ra Pathama and Wat P'ra Men.

The Thais, a people of the same stock as the Vietnamese, succeeded during the thirteenth century in dominating the Siam region. The extended exposure of the Thai people to the Mon-Khmer civilization had already left its mark in their embracement of Hinayana Buddhism. Once they had conquered the country, the Thais limited their efforts to spreading their own feudal organization and the Thai language (formerly called Siamese). Meanwhile, they were, of course, assimilating the Indianized culture of their new subjects. Increasingly, the Thais asserted themselves feudally at the expense of the Khmer Kingdom, which by now was well in decline, and they finally founded a new nation with its capital at Sukhodaya. History links its beginnings and growth to the name of Ram Kamheng (1281-1300), the monarch under whose rule the process of unification began. Later, the Thais of the Lop Buri region, the center of which was Ayuthia, succeeded in annexing Sukhodaya and conquering Angkor (1353). They would rule Siam until 1767, when they were finally defeated by the Burmese, who had been attacking them sporadically since the fifteenth century.

The earliest style we find in the Siam region is the Lop Buri, a twelfth-to-thirteenth century development of the Khmers. One example of the Lop Buri style is the Brah Prang Sam Yot, a Khmer sanctuary formed by three towers frontally aligned, located in the province for which this innovative style was named. Two interesting elements of this structure are the stucco decoration and the presence of human masks at the bases of its

columns. In the Wat Mahadhatu (Monastery of the Great Relic) at Lop Buri, the principal sanctuary is still inspired by the ogival tower at Angkor Wat, but displays considerable vertical thrust and rests on a high pedestal. An unmistakable desire for surface movement is apparent in the reduction and fragmentation of the structures; the interior cell has also become smaller, and its unique position on a very elevated pedestal makes it a true reliquary, inaccessible for direct worship.

The Wat Kukut at Lamphun, completed in 1218, more faithfully maintains the appearance of the Indianized art of the Dvaravati phase. It is a brick construction erected on a square base; and the five cubic bodies, progressively reduced in size, that rise in levels above this base are decorated on their faces by three niches containing images of Buddha. Furthermore, they display at each corner a bell-shaped structure that perhaps reproduces, on a reduced scale, the pinnacle in which the building must originally have terminated.

The socio-political structure of Siam was transformed under Thai domination, and inevitably the change was reflected in the artistic sphere. In the feudal society of the Thais, the chief—besides being lord and head of his family, of his vassals, and of the free men who owed him military service—had a religious authority that reinforced his political power, since it made him the ruling figure in the cult of the earth spirit, the *phi muong*. This tradition remotely echoed the Chinese system, and led to a form of royal cult very similar to that of the deified Khmer kings. It was not by accident that Ram Kamheng had placed on a hill near Sukhodaya the sacred image of a "Lord of the Summit," who rose above "all the spirits of the kingdom."[12]

The architecture of the Sukhodaya period abandons stone as its prime construction material and makes use of stucco-covered brick. A preference for two characteristic buildings is now manifest as well: the *prang* (or shrine), derived from the Khmer tower, is preceded by a hall with columns, which is covered by an imposing roof of wood and tiles. This hall, which contains the statue of Buddha, may even be large enough in size for use as a meeting place for monks. The second type is the stupa, often placed next to the sanctuary, in a form that either recalls the bell-shaped Indian structure transmitted from Burma or else imitates the tower-sanctuary of the Wat Kukut type. The structures and variations of the *prang* and the Thai stupa have their origin at Sukhodaya.

Among the other kinds of monuments we find, those of the commemorative type are exemplified in the Wat Mahadhatu at Sukhodaya, characterized by a slender tower terminating in a bulb.

Before the total unification of Siam was completed, the Thai kingdoms produced various regional schools, among which the Lan Na, which imitates Singhalese examples, should be mentioned. The founding of Ayuthia and the unification of the country marked the merging of the two artistic traditions on Siamese territory—the Thai and the Khmer. From the

282. Lamphun, Wat Kukut.
283. Lamphun, Wat Kukut, frontal
view (from Groslier, 1961).

284. Lop Buri, Wat Mahadhatu
(Monastery of the Great Relic).
285. Lop Buri, Brah Prang Sam
Yot.

beginning, the most important characteristic of this long phase was a return to Khmer models. Furthermore, the Thai rulers themselves would largely assimilate the organization of the Khmer court, an investiture that assumed, as we have noted, almost the nature of a deification. Of their old capital of Ayuthia, there remain today only slight traces of the foundations and brick walls of the palace. Still standing, however, are some of the ancient city's five hundred pagodas, which are scattered over the entire urban area. The southern part of the city once contained the royal chapel, or Wat P'ra Si Sanpet (fifteenth to eighteenth centuries), its nucleus formed by three large brick stupas in hemispherical form, covered in stucco and containing Buddhist relics; all three stupas had been placed on a terrace surrounded by a gallery.

In 1782, some years after the destruction of Ayuthia, a new capital was founded at Bangkok; the intent was to have it reproduce the appearance

of the capital city that had been destroyed. The royal palace allows us to verify the survival of certain architectural forms elaborated by the Thais. The Wat P'ra Keo, a Buddhist temple of precious stones, is formed by a sanctuary with a rectangular plan, with concave roofs and pronounced slopes, covered in brightly colored tiles. This type of roof is common to any meeting hall, whether it be the one intended for monks (*bot*) or that built for laymen (*vihan*); inside there may be only one nave or three. The statue of Buddha was placed at the end opposite the entrance. The Wat P'ra Keo is surrounded by a cloister; to the northwest a *chedi* (cetiya) was erected, in a bell form derived from the Singhalese stupa. It rises from a base surmounted by a small colonnade and a bell-shaped structure, on which rests the spire, composed of diminishing concentric rings. To the north, we find a *mondop* (mandapa), square in plan and formed by a cubic mass crowned by small diminishing levels and topped by a spire. Finally, to the northeast, there rises the temple where the statues of kings were preserved. It is a *prasat* derived from the Khmers, similar in its plan to a Greek cross, surmounted by superimposed roofs and enclosed by a slender *prang*—the final, stylized, Siamese result of the Khmer tower.

Laos

The first great Laotian kingdom was Lang Ch'ang, founded in the fourteenth century by Fa Ngum (1353-1373), who had grown up at Angkor and was the son-in-law of the king of Cambodia. Fa Ngum summoned a group of Khmer monks and craftsmen to his court immediately after his coronation, and the stable political order of the country that followed was the result of his initiative. A state emerged that hinged on two centers of culture: Luangprabang in the north, where the influence of the Chiengmai Thais and later of the Burmese was to prevail; and Vientiane, the southern city where the Khmer heritage would predominate and the artistic impact of Ayuthia would be most felt. The geographical structure of the region, constituted by the narrow Mekong Valley, hindered the formation of a truly unified society, and as a result the Thais of Laos never progressed beyond the stage of small feudal mountain principalities. The harsh realities of incessant internal struggles, particularly violent at the beginning of the eighteenth century, and wars with Burma and Siam, left little time for the development of art. We might say that the fall of Vieng Chan in 1778 and later destruction at the hands of the Siamese in 1828 constituted a blow that would still it for the time being.[13]

The art of this area is very akin to that of Siam, as is only natural, given the similar origin of the two peoples and their common religion—Hinayana Buddhism. The absence of a central political authority is especially reflected in its architecture, wherein the use of light and easily perishable materials predominated. As a result, remains are very scarce and do not allow us to follow in any complete fashion the development of this particular art. We can note, however, that its chief architectural types are: (1) the Buddhist

monastery or wat, in which the essential construction is the cult hall or meeting hall (*bot* or *vihan*); (2) the *th'at*, which replaces the stupa and is a reliquary connected to the wat; (3) the chapels and libraries similarly connected to the wat.

The tower-sanctuary (*prasat* or *kalan*), so widespread in Khmer and Cham art, is practically nonexistent in Laos; the divinity is offered to the devotion of the faithful in a building that combines the characteristics of a temple open to the worshiper and a shrine with walls and roof of brick. Moreover, while constructions in Java, Champa, and Cambodia are often very ancient, the oldest pagodas in Laos generally go back little more than two centuries. As for the absence of the tower-sanctuary, it seems strange that only Laos, among all Indianized countries, did not make use of this type of architecture. Parmentier[14] believes that the tower-sanctuary could not have been lacking in the Laotian wooden architecture of ancient times. It is his opinion that political conditions in the country prevented its being translated into stone, and that this is why no traces remain unless perhaps in the Wat Th'at in Luangprabang and in the *th'at* of the Wat Xtaphon at Muong Kuk.

Those constructions that have come down to us testify to the use of brickwork cut in large blocks, with the bricks being joined by means of a lime mortar. The vaulted roof was frequently used for small constructions; the saddle roof and the four-slope roof are characteristic of Laos. The so-called keel of the saddle roof is placed in accordance with the main axis of the hall, and the slopes descend to protrude beyond the walls. In the roof with four superimposed slopes, the two lower ones—which project considerably with respect to the four walls—rest on columns that form an actual gallery or veranda. Inside, the hall (or *vihan*) is divided into three naves; here the columns act to support the roof directly.

The *vihan*, which constitutes the basic part of the monastery, can be any one of the following: the simple hall, enclosed by a saddle roof; the hall with veranda, covered by a four-slope roof; and finally the hall with a circular nave, whose roof is supported by the outer wall. One or three approaching doors give access to the hall, which contains on an altar at the rear the statue of Buddha; an interior space was necessary for meetings between monks and the faithful. The *th'at*, which takes the place of the stupa or the chaitya, displays an extraordinary variety of solutions, but always the presence of common characteristics is easily discernible. The *th'at*, which is fully constructed in masonry, contains between its socle and top an element derived from the stupa that may vary in form from hemispherical to bell-shaped or bulbous.

The other architectural types that appear in Laos are chapels in masonry, and libraries, built of wood or sometimes of wood and brick, raised on a high socle.

The three styles that can be distinguished correspond to the three provinces into which the country is divided: (1) the Tran Ninh style, easily identified by the enormous lateral development of the roof and scant height

295. *Hoa-lu',* den *(dynastic temple)*
of Dinh.

296. *So'n-tay,* dinh *(temple of*
tutelary deity) of Chu-quyen.

297. *Hué, royal tombs of Nguyen,*
detail.

298. Hué, mausoleum of Emperor Tu'-du'c.
299. Hué, tomb of Emperor Minh-mang.

of the walls; (2) the Luangprabang style, distinctive for its lesser use of masonry and less imposing roofs; (3) the Vieng Chan style, characterized by high walls, roofs that are not especially ample, and vast halls.

We might examine in particular the Th'at Luang in Vieng Chan, which is also important for its antiquity (it was founded in 1586). The temple, which imitates contemporary structures in Siam, is erected on an enclosed base. The mass of the stupa, constituted by a hemispherical section on a square base, ends at its four corners in elegant spires, supported by a band of lotus petals. The base of the stupa is surrounded by buildings on a reduced scale, reproducing the base of the stupa, which develops outward. The enclosure is constituted by a cloister, opening on each side into chapels, with the southern one serving as an entrance to the gallery. The outer cloister of the full perimeter wall opened on its four sides into four pavilions.

Vietnam

Archaeological findings in Vietnam begin from around the fourth century B.C. with a wealth of bronze art. Its most important traces, bronze drums that show an obvious Chinese influence, have been found in the Dong-Son area. The Tonkin Delta was a Chinese colony until the tenth century, a subjugation that not only gave the country its social and economic structure but also profoundly influenced its art. According to Vietnamese tradition, two kingdoms—both partly legendary—existed at the beginning of the country's history. The first, known as Xichquy, extended northward as far as the Blue River; the second, Van-lang, more or less corresponded to the actual Tonkin. The first historical kingdom, Au-lac, falls between 257 and 208 B.C. Its capital, Co-lao, has been unearthed, in the form of an immense enclosure whose imposing vestiges have not yet been fully explored.

From 214 B.C. to A.D. 938 Tonkin, divided into three border regions, formed part of the Chinese Empire and felt its influence not only politically but culturally as well. The official language of the area was Chinese, which contributed decisively to making its culture even more Chinese. When a system of dams (built in a series of successive divisions) was created in the delta to encourage agricultural development, Chinese rule was thus established *ense et aratro*—by the sword and the plowshare. This irrigation system, with its series of diminishing basins, and its canals dividing the land geometrically into units and hamlets, indissolubly bound the Vietnamese to the needs imposed by this means of exploiting the soil, since such installations had to be constantly controlled. It also determined the structure of the Vietnamese village, a unit complete in itself, and capable of drawing all its subsistence from the rice fields.

There persisted, however, a deeply rooted cult of earth spirits, a fundamental religious element on which official Confucianism had little effect. The political structure of the country was that of a pyramid, with the Chinese emperor at the top; the least sign of weakness in the central power was accompanied by a breakdown in the political-administrative structure

300. Hué, tower of the Linh Mu pagoda.

of the territory itself. The history of Vietnam is thus not the history of an empire or an ideology, but of small cells of farmers in search of arable land, who are prepared to move for that purpose with the support of the soldiers of the central power.[15]

In the tenth century the national Dinh dynasty (A.D. 868-980), taking advantage of the decadence of the T'ang emperors, seized power. One of its characteristics, as was true also of later dynasties, was a push toward the south, a drive that arose from Vietnamese cultivation of the lowlands. The people remained tied to the aforementioned cult of earth spirits, but since they were cut off from the sphere of Indianization, the king and the aristocratic class devoted themselves to Confucianism and Taoism.

At the beginning, there was no architecture to speak of—even though luxury objects worthy indeed of the name of art were produced—until the great fervor of Mahayana Buddhism spread into Vietnam from the China of the Six Dynasties and the T'ang. This new development gave rise during the ninth century to important monasteries, of which unfortunately almost nothing remains today. The terraced tower of Binh Son (Vinh-yen) was built under the Li dynasty during the twelfth century. It is adorned with terra-cotta coverings and medallions inspired by Chinese models of the period.

By 1225 the Vietnamese had begun to prevail over the Chams. Although they were arrested first by the Mongol menace, then by the Ming annexation of Tonkin, they finally succeeded in reasserting themselves as an independent force and annexed all of Champa. Under the Le dynasty (fifteenth to eighteenth centuries), they were truly successful in creating an empire. The Nguyen dynasty that was established in the year 1801, once it had resolved problems of internal opposition and resistance and unified the country, turned against the Thais. The French conquest of Indochina put an end to Vietnamese attempts at a total encirclement of Indianized Indochina.

Architecturally, the period of the Le dynasty proved to be the richest, and fortunately a great many of its works remain to attest the Vietnamese reworking of Chinese themes and elements. The most important of these are the royal tombs at Lam-so'n and the buildings at Hoa-lu'.

Of the art of the Nguyen dynasty, which begins in the nineteenth century with Gialong, its founder and first ruler, numerous architectural works remain. Except for the palace halls in Hué, they are all of a religious nature. Four types of buildings can be distinguished: the *dinh*, or temple of the tutelary deity of the village; the *chua*, or Buddhist temple; the *den*, or Taoist dynastic temple; and the *van-mieu*, or temple of Confucius. Each building is of wood, with a framework supported by columns that rest without being embedded on stone socles fixed in the ground. Their fundamental characteristic is their natural setting, the framing of the work by the landscape.

The *dinh*, built on piles, appears to recall the houses represented on the Dong-Son drums mentioned earlier. In this building the notables received visitors, deliberated on questions of common interest, and sacrificed to the tutelary deity; here literary contests and social life took place.[16] It is generally composed of two parallel wings—the rear one constructed with a forepart at its center that holds the altar of the guardian spirit—and large halls for banquets and meetings. Adjacent buildings contain kitchens and a place for animal sacrifice.

The form of the *chua* can best be described as that of an H lying on its side, surrounded on three sides by loggias and by a courtyard on the fourth. The H-shaped part comprises the actual sanctuary, the incense hall, and the hall where the faithful assemble, while the loggias and courtyard contain statues of bonzes (Buddhist monks). Outwardly, the *den* is similar to the *chua*, but inside a statue or symbol is enclosed in a shrine that is impossible to enter. The *van-mieu*, dedicated to Confucius, is a vast complex of buildings arranged within an enclosure.

The imperial palace complex in Hué, built by Gialong and showing a strong Chinese influence, deserves particular mention. The Hué complex is constructed in obedience to all the geomantic rituals that were thought to ensure the presence of beneficent influences for the dignitary whose home it would be. Surrounded by hills to protect its gates from evil spirits, the palace is a series of enclosures that increasingly diminish until one reaches the Throne Room, heart of the construction and of the empire itself. Each courtyard contains a reconstruction in miniature of the entire universe, a microcosm of rocks, trees, and lakes. The architectural structure of the Hué complex does not allow itself to be deciphered; to gain knowledge of it would be tantamount to controlling it magically. We are indebted to Groslier for his excellent interpretation: "In fact the imperial residence would seem to be an ideogram written on the earth by the Emperor-Organizer of the world, for the eyes alone of the Emperor of Heaven, from whom he has received his powers."[17]

Arcangela Santoro

301. *Hué, imperial city; in the background, the Throne Room.*
302. *Hanoi, the Van-mieu (Temple of Literature).*

NOTES

INTRODUCTION

[1] Kautilya in the *Arthaśastra*, the principal text of political theory in India, warns that one of the most serious dangers a sovereign can incur is that of allowing the *śrenī* to flourish. If these guilds are too powerful, an eventual clash with them may lead to the collapse of the system and the fall of the sovereign.

[2] Cf. J. Gernet, "Notes sur les villes chinoises au moment de l'apogée islamique," *The Islamic City*, edited by A.H. Houtrani and S.M. Stern, Oxford, 1970, pp. 77 ff.

[3] Jean Chesneaux, "Le Mode de production asiatique: une nouvelle étape de la discussion," *Eirene*, III, 1964, and "Récents Travaux marxistes sur le mode de production asiatique," *La Pensée*, 114, 1964.

[4] Asia was the first to use nickel for coins (the Indo-Grecian and Greco-Bactrian kingdoms) and paper money (used in China), and later would even use clay *fiches* for coins of scant value (as did Thailand in the eighteenth and nineteenth centuries).

Chapter One

INDIA AND CEYLON

[1] Cf. J. Auboyer, *Introduction à l'étude de l'art de l'Inde*, Rome, Is.M.E.O., 1965, pp. 59 ff.

[2] Indeed, there seem to be traces of conduits (unfinished) designed for this purpose. On the other hand, it was thought at first—as Father Heras also pointed out—that the trench was meant to be eroded away, widened, and open at least on the side facing the valley.

[3] Cf. M. Bussagli and C. Sivaramamurti, *5000 Years of the Art of India*, New York, 1971.

[4] Note that bricks change dimensions and consistency according to the period, as can be seen in the following tabulation: the average dimensions of a brick in the Maurya period—height or thickness 2 inches, length 19 5/8 inches, width 12 1/4 inches; at Sanchi (Stupa 1, second century B.C.)—height 3 inches, length 16 inches, width 10 inches; at Mathura (second century A.D.)—height 3 inches (also maintained elsewhere until the eighth century and beyond), length 13 5/8 inches (but also 10 7/8), width 10 1/4 or 8 1/2 inches. In later temples, especially those of Orissa, the dimensions are less (height 3 inches, length 13 inches, width 10 1/4 inches).

[5] Cf. C. Sivaramamurti, *Sanskrit Literature and Art, Mirrors of Indian Culture*, M.A.S.I., No. 73, Calcutta, 1955, which mentions in this regard the verses of the *Rāmāyana* (V. 2.23; repeated 3.32) in which a temple is compared to the crests of the Kailasa grazing the sky; the same image recurs in a commemorative inscription. Similarly, the comparison with Mount Meru, the cosmic mountain, recurs both in the *Rāmāyana* and in commemorative inscriptions in the south. In other cases, however, the reference is to gigantic beings (such as elephants), clouds, and cosmic changes. All this has nothing to do with the technical texts. The *Mānasāra*, the *Purānas*, and the *Śilpas* are followed by a great many other such works that indicate rules, measures, and techniques—all directed to obtaining aesthetically valid, and in their way functional, forms. They do not, however, dwell on the effect of *rāsa* that the work may arouse in the beholder.

[6] The *samgha*, or Buddhist community, is, along with Buddha and the Law he preaches, one of the Three Jewels—that is, one of the essential pillars on which this religion is founded.

[7] E. Lamotte, *Histoire du Bouddhisme indien des origines à l'ère Saka*, Louvain, 1958, pp. 365-66.

[8] Cf. A. Volwahsen, *Living Architecture: Indian*, New York, 1969, pp. 144 ff.

[9] Cf. J. Auboyer, *op. cit.*, p. 84.

[10] Cf. *Epigraphia Indica*, I, p. 159. The inscription in copper is reproduced in Plates 104 and 105.

[11] S. Kramrisch, *The Art of India*, London, 1954.

Chapter Two

INDONESIA AND INDOCHINA

[1] M. Bussagli, "India Esteriore," *Enciclopedia Universale dell'Arte*, VII, Rome-Venice, 1958, col. 318.

[2] *Ibid.*, col. 326.

[3] C. Holt, *Art in Indonesia*, New York, 1967, p. 5.

[4] *Ibid.*, p. 39.

[5] J.G. de Casparis, *Prasasti Indonesia*, I, Bandung, 1950, pp. 160-92.

[6] M. Hallade, *L'Asie du Sud est*, Paris, 1954, p. 5.

[7] B.P. Groslier, *Indocina*, Milan, 1961, pp. 56-57.

[8] *Ibid.*, p. 105.

[9] *Ibid.*, p. 147.

[10] G. Coedès, "Birmania, centri e tradizioni," *Enciclopedia Universale dell'Arte*, II, col. 605.

[11] *Ibid.*, col. 607.

[12] Groslier, *op. cit.*, p. 230.

[13] G. Coedès, "Arte dell'Indonesia," *Civiltà dell'Oriente*, IV, Rome, 1962, p. 943.

[14] H. Parmentier, *L'Art du Laos*, Paris, 1954, pp. 3-4.

[15] Groslier, *op. cit.*, pp. 40-42.

[16] *Ibid.*, pp. 252-54.

[17] *Ibid.*, p. 254.

(The abbreviations *E.U.A.* and *B.E.F.E.O.* stand for *Enciclopedia Universale dell'Arte* and *Bulletin de l'Ecole Française de l'Extrême-Orient*, respectively).

INDIA

ACHARYA P.K.; *Indian Architecture According to Mānasāra-Śilpaśāstra*, 3 vols. London 1927-46.

AUBOYER J., *Introduction à l'étude de l'art de l'Inde*, Rome 1965.

AUBOYER J. and ZANNAS E., *Khajuraho*, The Hague 1960.

BATLEY C., *The Design Development of Indian Architecture*, 2nd ed. London 1948.

BEHARI DUTT B., *Town Planning in Ancient India*, Calcutta 1925.

BOSE N.H., *Canons of Orissan Architecture*, Calcutta 1932.

BROWN P., *Indian Architecture*, Vol. I: *Buddhist and Hindu Periods*, 3rd ed. Bombay 1961.

BUSSAGLI M., and SIVARAMAMURTI C., *5000 Years of Indian Art*, New York 1971.

COOMARASWAMY A.K., A *History of Indian and Indonesian Art*, London-New York 1927.

COOMARASWAMY A.K., "Indian Architectural Terms," *The American Oriental Society Journal*, 48, 1928, pp. 250-75.

COUSENS H., *Somanatha and Other Medieval Temples of Kathiawād*, Calcutta 1931.

FERGUSSON J., *A History of Indian and Eastern Architecture*, London 1876.

FERGUSSON J., and BURGESS J., *Cave Temples of India*, London 1880.

FOUCHER A., *L'Art gréco-bouddhique du Gandhāra*, 4 vols., Paris 1905-51.

GRAVELY F.H., *An Outline of Indian Temple Architecture*, Bombay 1954.

HAVELL E.B., *The Ancient and Medieval Architecture of India: A Study of Indo-Aryan Civilisation*, London 1915.

JOUVEAU-DUBREUIL G., *L'Archéologie du sud de l'Inde*, 2 vols., Paris 1914.

KAK R.C., *Ancient Monuments of Kashmir*, London 1933.

KRAMRISCH S., *The Hindu Temple*, 2 vols., Calcutta 1946.

LONGHURST A.H., *Pallava Architecture*, 3 vols., Calcutta 1924-30.

MARCHAL H., *L'Architecture comparée dans l'Inde et l'Extrême-Orient*, Paris 1944.

MARSHALL J. and FOUCHER A., *The Monuments of Sañchi*, 3 vols., New Delhi 1939.

RAMACHANDRAN T.N., "Tiruparuttikunram and Its Temples," *Bulletin of Madras Government Museum*, New Series, General Section, III, 1934.

RANGACHARI K., "Town-planning and House-building in Ancient India According to Śilpaśāstra," *Indian Historical Quarterly*, December 1927 and March 1928.

RENON L., "La Maison vedique," *Journal Asiatique*, CCXXI, 1939, pp. 481 ff.

ROWLAND B., *The Art and Architecture of India*, 2nd ed. Baltimore 1956.

SARABHAJ N., *Jain Tirthas and Their Architecture*, Ahmedabad, 1944.

SASTRI K.A., "The Economy of a South Indian Temple (Tanjore) in the Cola Period," *Malaviya Commemorative Volume*, Madras 1932, pp. 302 ff.

SIVARAMAMURTI C., "Sanskrit Literature and Art: Mirrors of Indian Culture," *Memoirs of the Archaeological Survey of India*, Vol. 73, Calcutta-New Delhi 1955.

SMITH V.A., A *History of Fine Art in India and Ceylon*, 2nd ed. (revised by K. de B. Codrington), Oxford 1930.

VOLWAHSEN A., *Living Architecture: Indian*, New York 1969.

ZIMMER H., *The Art of Indian Asia*, 2 vols., New York 1955.

CEYLON

"*Mahavamsa,*" *or the Great Chronicle of Ceylon*, Translation by Wilhelm Geiger. Published under the auspices of the Ceylon Government Information Department, Colombo 1950.

PARANAVITANA S., *Art and Architecture of Ceylon: Polonnaruva Period*, Colombo (?) 1954.

PARANAVITANA S., "Ceylon, correnti e tradizioni," *E.U.A.*, III, Rome-Venice 1958, cols. 420-28.

PARANAVITANA S., *Encyclopedia of Buddhism (Volume of Specimen Articles): Architecture (Ceylon)*. Published under the auspices of the Department of Cultural Affairs, Government of Ceylon. Colombo 1957.

PARANAVITANA S., *The Stupa in Ceylon*, Colombo 1946.

SMITHER J.G., *Architectural Remains of Anuradhapura*, Colombo 1877.

INDONESIA AND INDOCHINA

General Works

BUSSAGLI M., "India Esteriore," *E.U.A.*, VII, Rome-Venice 1958, cols. 318-37.

COEDÈS G., "Arte dell'Indonesia," *Civiltà dell'Oriente*, Vol. IV, Rome 1962.

COEDÈS G., *Les Etats hindouisés d'Indochine et d'Indonésie*, Paris 1948.

GROSLIER B.P., *Indocina*, Milan 1961.

HALLADE M., *L'Asie du Sud est*, Paris 1954.

MARCHAL H., *L'Architecture comparée dans l'Inde et l'Extrême-Orient*, Paris 1944.

MASPERO P., *Un Empire colonial français: l'Indochine*, 2 vols., Paris 1929-30.

PARMENTIER H., *L'Art architectural hindou dans l'Inde et l'Extrême-Orient*, Paris 1948.

Indonesia

BERNET KEMPERS A.J., *Ancient Indonesian Art*, Cambridge (Mass.) 1959.

HEINE-GELDERN R. VON and HALLADE M., "Indonesia, culture e tradizioni," *E.U.A.*, VII, Rome-Venice 1958, cols. 453-502.

HOLT C., *Art in Indonesia*, New York 1967.

LOHUIZEN-DE LEEUW J.E. VAN and TADDEI M., "Arte dell'Indonesia," *Civiltà dell'Oriente*, Vol. IV, Rome 1962.

MUS P., "Esquisse d'une histoire du bouddhisme fondée sur la critique archéologique des textes," *B.E.F.E.O.*, XXXII, 1932, pp. 269-439; XXXIII, 1933, pp. 577-980; XXXIV, 1934, pp. 175-400.

SARKAR H.B., *Some Contributions of India to the Ancient Civilization of Indonesia and Malaysia*, Calcutta 1970.

SIVARAMAMURTI C., *Le Stupa de Barobudur*, Paris 1960.

WAGNER F.A., *Indonesia: The Art of an Island Group*, New York 1959.

Cambodia (the Khmers) and Champa

BÉNISTI M., *Rapports entre le premier art Khmer e l'art Indien*, 2 vols., Paris 1970.

BOISSELIER J., *Le Cambodge, Manuel d'archéologie d'Extrême-Orient, Asie du Sud est*, Vol. I, Paris 1966.

BOSCH F.D., "Le Temple d'Angkor Vat," *B.E.F.E.O.*, XXXII, 1923, pp. 7-21.

COEDÈS G., "Cambogia," *E.U.A.*, III, Rome-Venice, 1958, cols. 69-79.

COEDÈS G., "Cham, scuola," *E.U.A.*, III, Rome-Venice 1958, cols. 446-51.

COEDÈS G., "Etudes cambodgiennes XXIII: La date du temple de Bantay Srei," *B.E.F.E.O.*, XXIX, 1929, pp. 289-96.

COEDÈS G., "Khmer, centri e tradizioni," *E.U.A.*, VIII, Rome-Venice 1958, cols. 454-71.

CORAL-RÉMUSAT G. DE, *L'Art Khmèr, les grandes étapes de son évolution*, Paris 1940.

DUFOUR H. and CARPEAUX C., *Le Bayon d'Angkor Thom*, Paris 1910.

DUMARÇAIS J., *Le Bayon: Histoire architecturale du temple*, Paris 1967.

FILLIOZAT J., "Le Symbolisme du monument du Phnom Bakheng," *B.E.F.E.O.*, XLIV, 1954, pp. 527-54.

FINOT L., GOLOUBEW V. and COEDÈS G., *Le Temple d'Angkor Vat*, 7 vols., Paris 1929-32.

GROSLIER B.P. and ARTHAUD J., *The Arts and Civilization of Angkor*, rev. ed. New York 1966.

LEUBA J., *Les Chams et leur art*, Paris-Brussels 1923.

MASPERO P., *Le Royaume de Champa*, Paris 1928.

MAZZEO D., and SILVI ANTONINI C., *Civiltà Khmer*, Milan 1972.

PARMENTIER H., *L'Art Khmèr classique*, Paris 1939.

PARMENTIER H., "La Construction dans l'architecture Khmère classique," *B.E.F.E.O.*, XXXV, 1935, pp. 243-309.

STERN P., *L'Art du Champa et son évolution*, Toulouse 1942.

STERN P., *Le Bayon d'Angkor Thom et l'évolution de l'art Khmèr*, Paris 1927.

Burma and Siam (Thailand)

CLAEYS J.Y., "L'Archéologie du Siam," *B.E.F.E.O.*, XXXI, 1931, pp. 361-448.

COEDÈS G., "Birmania, centri e tradizioni," *E.U.A.*, II, Rome-Venice 1959, cols. 604-13.

DUPONT P., *L'Archéologie mône de Dvaravati*, 2 vols., Paris 1959.

GRISWOLD A.B., "Siamese, scuola," *E.U.A.*, XII, Rome-Venice 1964, cols. 453-62.

GRISWOLD A.B., "Thailandia," *E.U.A.*, XIII, Rome-Venice, 1965, cols. 528-43.

GRISWOLD A.B., KIM C. and POTT P.H., *Birmania, Corea, Tibet*, Milan 1963.

LE MAY R.S., *A Concise History of Buddhist Art In Siam*, 2nd ed. Rutland-Tokyo 1963.

Laos and Vietnam

BEZACIER L., *L'Art vietnamien*, Paris 1934.

BEZACIER L., *Relevé des monuments du Viet-nam*, Paris 1959.

BEZACIER L., "Vietnamiti centri e scuole," *E.U.A.*, XIV, Rome-Venice 1966, cols. 809-22.

COEDÈS G., "Laos, scuola," *E.U.A.*, VIII, Rome-Venice 1958, cols. 536-42.

MALLERET L., *L'Archéologie du delta du Mekong*, 6 vols., Paris 1959-63.

MERCIER R. and PARMENTIER H., "Eléments anciens d'architecture au Nord Vietnam," *B.E.F.E.O.*, XLV, 1952, pp. 285-348.

NGUEN VAN KHOAN, "Essai sur le dinh," *B.E.F.E.O.*, XXX, 1930, pp. 107-12.

PARMENTIER H., *L'Art du Laos*, 2 vols., Paris 1954.

PARMENTIER H., *Inventaire descriptif des monuments cham de l'Annam*, 2 vols., Paris 1909.

TRAN-HAM-TAN, "Etude sur le Van mieu (temple de la littérature) de Ha-noi," *B.E.F.E.O.*, XLV, 1951-52, pp. 89-117.

LIST OF PHOTOGRAPHIC CREDITS
The numbers refer to the plates

Archaeological Survey of India, Government of India: 2, 3, 4, 7, 8, 9, 11, 12, 13, 19, 28, 33, 34, 36, 37, 38, 56, 75, 87, 88, 89, 90, 97, 98, 99, 117, 118, 123, 138, 139, 143, 145, 178.

Borromeo, Federico, Milan: I, II, III, IV, V, VI, VII, VIII, IX, X, XI, XII, XIII, XIV, XV, XIX, XX, XXII, XXIII, XIV

Carrà, Luca, Milan: XVI, XVII, XVIII

Ecole Française d'Extrême-Orient, Paris: 224, 253, 255, 256, 257, 291, 292, 295, 296, 298, 302

Missi-Photo, Paris: 297, 299, 300, 301, 303

Service Archéologique d'Indonesie, Paris: 218

Stierlin, Henri, Geneva; 226, 229, 230, 231, 232, 235, 236, 240, 241, 242, 243, 244, 248, 249, 250, 251, 252, XXI